Organizing Information in School Libraries

Organizing Information in School Libraries

Basic Principles and New Rules

Cynthia Houston

LIBRARIES
UNLIMITED™
An Imprint of ABC-CLIO, LLC
Santa Barbara, California • Denver, Colorado

Library of Congress Cataloging-in-Publication Data

Names: Houston, Cynthia, author.
Title: Organizing information in school libraries : basic principles and new rules /
    Cynthia Houston.
Description: Santa Barbara, CA : Libraries Unlimited, an imprint of ABC-CLIO,
    LLC, [2016] | Includes index.
Identifiers: LCCN 2015025228| ISBN 9781440836862 (paperback) |
    ISBN   9781440836879 (ebook)
Subjects: LCSH: Cataloging. | School libraries. | BISAC: LANGUAGE ARTS &
    DISCIPLINES / Library & Information Science / Cataloging & Classification. |
    LANGUAGE ARTS & DISCIPLINES / Library & Information Science / School
    Media.
Classification: LCC Z693 .H685 2016 | DDC 025.3—dc23 LC record available at
    http://lccn.loc.gov/2015025228

ISBN: 978-1-4408-3686-2
EISBN: 978-1-4408-3687-9

20   19   18   17   16   1   2   3   4   5

This book is also available on the World Wide Web as an eBook.
Visit www.abc-clio.com for details.

Libraries Unlimited
An Imprint of ABC-CLIO, LLC

ABC-CLIO, LLC
130 Cremona Drive, P.O. Box 1911
Santa Barbara, California 93116-1911

This book is printed on acid-free paper ∞
Manufactured in the United States of America

This book honors the members of the Kentucky Association of School Librarians, an organization filled with powerful, dedicated, and passionate educational leaders and teacher-librarians.

Contents

Introduction

Organizing Information in School Libraries: Basic Principles and New Rules is intended for librarians in school and small public libraries who are rich in patrons and short on staff. Designed to assist solo librarians with multiple responsibilities, this book introduces basic principles and streamlined procedures for cataloging library materials as efficiently as possible, so that the focus of their work is on meeting the information needs of users, first and foremost.

Instructors in school library education programs can use this book as a teaching tool for introducing the basic concepts, principles, and procedures for classification and cataloging of library materials in an easy-to-understand manner. The initial chapters discuss the ever-changing world of library automation and innovations that allow a wide variety of print and electronic materials to be included in the library catalog. Chapters also explain the basic concepts related to library catalogs, subject analysis, and classification, with exercises designed to help students apply new knowledge to practical problems. The final chapters provide step-by-step procedures, examples, and practice exercises for cataloging print, realia, audiovisual, and Internet materials using the new Resource Description and Access (RDA) standards.

As the book is intended for novice catalogers, it provides a very brief introduction to the *Abridged Dewey Decimal Classification* and the subfields of the Machine Readable Cataloging Record (MARC) record. Cataloging instructors may want to delve into these topics in more detail using their own course materials. Additionally, the book does not discuss the *Anglo American Cataloging Rules* (AACR) in any detail, as novice catalogers are not familiar with these standards, and will be applying RDA standards when they are creating new records, or editing records obtained from other catalog record providers.

Cataloging has been both a challenge and joy for me throughout my years in the library media education field. My attempts to make the complex subject matter of classification, subject analysis, descriptive cataloging, automated cataloging, and call number building understandable for my students have resulted in the educational materials included in this book. It is my hope that cataloging will be a less daunting and more streamlined process for the present and future school librarians who use this book.

Acknowledgments

A world of thanks goes to my family, particularly my husband, Jim, who patiently listened to my explanation of the nuances of ISBD punctuation. Many thanks go to my colleagues in the Library Media Education program at Western Kentucky University, particularly Dr. Barbara Fiehn, whose wealth of knowledge and experience in administering the school library program has contributed to the shape and character of this book.

1

The World of the Library Catalog

INTRODUCTION

Imagine that you are a librarian touring a farm with school-age children. Suddenly, one of them stops in front of a pen holding a very cute baby pig. Reading your student's expression of yearning, you retrieve your smart phone and speak into the microphone: "What information does my library have on potbellied pigs as pets?" You are instantly connected to a list of print and electronic information on potbellied pigs. A voice on your phone says, "Our library has 3 books, 10 articles, 1 video, and 14 websites on potbellied pigs as pets. Please select the resources you are interested in from the list." After a quick review of the information, you turn and say to the child, "Honey, in a few years, that little thing will grow into a full-size pig, much too big for your home." You show the child a picture of a full-size potbellied pig as proof of your statement.

This scenario illustrates the ideal library catalog—one that is ubiquitous, user-friendly, and provides authoritative and complete information on a topic using simple search queries and natural language. Although many of us are already accessing information from the Internet on our mobile devices in this manner, very few library catalogs are this sophisticated. Historically, the purpose of a library catalog was to provide an inventory of the library's physical holdings, which was accessible only to the librarian who retrieved the items at the request of the library user. Today, library catalogs and the information they organize are no longer the sole province of the librarian, but using them often feels awkward because they were originally developed by and for librarians as opposed to library users.

In the 21st century, users have expectations about their information search experiences and bring these expectations to the library when they have information needs. Users expect library catalog searching to be similar to their Internet searches—user-friendly, with natural language, and a list of relevant results. Additionally, they have higher expectations for library catalogs because users believe that results from a catalog search will be more relevant and authoritative than an Internet search (Casey, 2007). Fulfilling users' expectations for a library catalog to provide instantaneously available, relevant, and high-quality resources has been elusive for 21st-century librarians and may be one of the biggest challenges facing libraries today. Developing the ideal library catalog would require that librarians on the local, national, and international levels collaborate in an effort to make the entire world of information, regardless of format, readily available to be retrieved anywhere and anytime.

UNIVERSAL BIBLIOGRAPHIC CONTROL

The issue described earlier is one librarians refer to as "universal bibliographic control" and centers on the challenge of curating an ever-growing and ever-changing bibliographic universe. The "bibliographic universe" is the term used to describe all the recorded knowledge in existence. In the past, when physical writings were not common and used primarily to record the comings and goings of the ruling class, the library contained most of the bibliographic universe their users required in its local facility. To organize and store these writings, libraries were developed, and librarians became the "keepers" of these collections. The professional training of librarians concerned how to best organize these collections for their own access. The focus of a librarian's task was maintaining a descriptive list of library items, called a catalog. As the catalog list grew when the bibliographic universe expanded, items were arranged into similar groups or "classes" based on notions of how the universe was organized. The librarian's task of organizing items into these groups became known as "classification" (Chan, 2007).

Classification and cataloging were the chief functions of professional librarians for centuries, because until the early 20th century, libraries contained much of the printed bibliographic universe. In the early 19th century, libraries initially were privately owned or were a members-only institution, restricted to scholars and members of the ruling class. When public libraries were created in the late 19th and early 20th centuries, the collection was not available directly to the public. A professional librarian would retrieve items from the collection at the users' request from the "closed stacks." In later years, public and academic libraries opened their "stacks," and users were able to use the card catalog to locate items for themselves (Taylor, 2004).

When the library stacks were opened to the public later in the 20th century, the function of the library catalog to help users find information became very important. Support structures for helping libraries across the country to develop and maintain their catalogs were a key function of the Library of Congress Card Catalog Service. This service, along with the Cataloging in Publication service provided by the Library of Congress, made the card catalog the premier information discovery tool for almost a hundred years (Taylor, 2004).

The large wooden card catalog was part and parcel of every school library across the country when school libraries became commonplace in the mid-20th century. As part of improving math and science education during the Cold War, the National Defense Education Act of 1958 brought a trove of resources to schools in the math and science areas that required organization. This act was the initial step in bringing libraries and library resources to schools. Later, the National Elementary and Secondary Education Act, passed in 1965, brought another wealth of resources to schools related to promoting literacy. Across the country, school libraries were installed in elementary, middle, and secondary schools, with professional school librarians to manage the collection (Michie & Holton, 2005).

Up until the late 20th century, school librarians primarily curated their local collections, which included maintaining and updating the card catalog and ensuring that the collection was in the proper order on the shelves. Now, times have changed. With the advent of multimedia electronic technology and the Internet, the amount of recorded knowledge in the bibliographic universe has expanded far beyond the library walls and librarians' organizational capacities. Because of the increase in the availability and popularity of eBooks, periodical databases, and multimedia information resources, a significant portion of the physical collection of the library has given way to the virtual collection. In many schools, the "warehouse" model of school libraries comprised primarily of books and library shelving has been transformed to a "learning commons," where students access information electronically using mobile devices. Consequently, the school librarian's job of curating the library collection has also transformed into that of instructional partner, information guide, and technology leader (Loertscher, Koechlin, & Zwaan, 2011).

ORGANIZATION OF THE BIBLIOGRAPHIC UNIVERSE

Given our limitless access to information in the 21st century, are libraries really needed? Many would say that because the bibliographic universe is so large and disorganized, the traditional classification and cataloging functions of the librarian are more important than ever. For in such a chaotic electronic information world, information specialists will be critical for maintaining order and access.

In this day and age, libraries exist in two worlds: (1) the physical world of books, audiovisual materials, and periodicals housed on the library shelves; and (2) the virtual world of the electronic catalog or Online Public Access Catalog (OPAC), electronic periodical databases, and electronic resources available for users to download. The ordered world of the physical library contains fiction and nonfiction items, periodicals, and biographical information in print and audiovisual formats. The virtual items in the library include eBooks, electronic periodicals, and digital archives, which although not physically present in the library building are an important part of the library collection. All of these items can be found in the automated library catalog, which directs users to where they can be found in the library.

In a physical library, users can search for items in the library catalog by subject, author, title, or keyword using the OPAC and find their exact location on the shelf by "call number." Users can also browse the library shelves, because the classification systems used for fiction and nonfiction arrange items in a logical and consistent order. In many libraries, the virtual library is also accessed through the OPAC and contains links to electronic databases, websites, and other electronic media the library offers patrons in the virtual world.

A premier example of a 21st-century information discovery tool is WorldCat, which links to the collections of more than 10,000 libraries across the globe. WorldCat was developed and is maintained by the Online Computer Library Center (OCLC), a nonprofit cooperative of libraries that share technology tools and resources. Using WorldCat, users can search for physical and virtual items using the same search interface. Figure 1.1 shows search options and results of a WorldCat search.

Note that in a search for information on *Alice in Wonderland*, options include searching by title, subject, and keyword. The results list displays thousands of titles in a large number of different formats including print books, articles, audiovisual materials, and websites. An additional feature of WorldCat is its ability to link the information in the results list to the holdings of local libraries. So, for example, selecting one of the

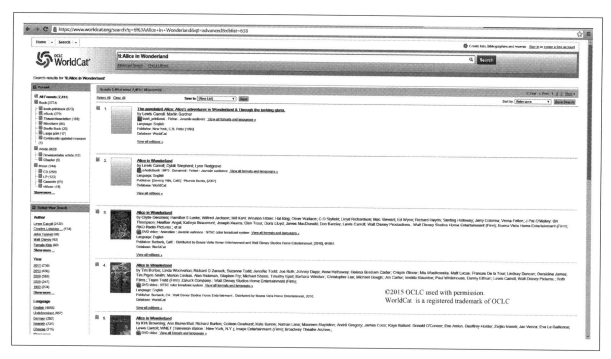

©2015 OCLC used with permission.
WorldCat is a registered trademark of OCLC

Figure 1.1. WorldCat search interface

resources on the results list shows whether the item is held by any libraries in proximity to a specific zip code. This is an example of how physical and virtual library holdings that represent the bibliographic universe can be found in one information source.

CREATING THE LIBRARY CATALOG

All automated catalogs contain records created by catalogers. When looking at the details in a catalog record, information about the items' "intellectual contents" and location on the library shelf is listed. This information is the result of a complex process of classification and cataloging using a number of different sets of rules, procedures, and online resources. The main tasks involved in the classification and cataloging process include describing the intellectual contents of the item using a specific set of subject descriptors and assigning the item to a location on the shelf based on its academic discipline or "class." Broken down into a step-by-step process, classification and cataloging involve the following procedures:

1. Description—creating a descriptive record for an item in a library catalog based on professional standards.
2. Subject cataloging—assigning subject terms that describe the most important facets of an item using a standard list of subject terms otherwise known as a "controlled vocabulary."
3. Classification—assigning an item to a specific class of items based on their common features typically using a classification scheme such as the Dewey Decimal Classification (DDC).

4. Assigning a call number—creating a unique number for each item using a notation system that combines the item's classification, publication date, and sometimes a "Cutter number," which is a code created from the first letters of an author's surname. (Taylor, 2000)

When we use an information discovery tool such as WorldCat and we see records displayed in a uniform format, we never think about how the millions of records are created or maintained. These records are developed by catalogers who create all the information contained in a catalog record, including descriptive information about the item being cataloged, subject terms describing the item, and a classification number using either the Dewey Decimal or Library of Congress Classification (LCC) schemes. The classification and cataloging activities completed for these records are typically done in the technical services area of an academic or public library, by a vendor of library records, by cooperative cataloging services, or the Library of Congress. In a public or academic library, different people may be involved in these tasks because often classification and cataloging for technical or academic subjects involve specialized knowledge and expertise in how these items are cataloged. In a school library, these records are typically purchased when the item is purchased, copied from another library catalog, or created by the school librarian based on accepted cataloging and classification standards and procedures.

STANDARDIZING THE LIBRARY CATALOG

When using an automated catalog, users expect to see records displayed in a manner that is consistent, complete, and correct in their description of the item. An important feature of a catalog's usability is that all records are displayed using the same format and include the same types of information, such as the author, title, publication date, and publisher. Being able to look at records from libraries across the world and seeing them displayed in the same format are the results of international standardized policies and procedures for library catalogs (Taylor, 2004).

One of the most useful services provided for librarians by the Library of Congress is the Cataloging in Publication Program (CIP), which provides classification and cataloging information for titles selected for the Library of Congress collection. Titles from U.S. publishers that the Library of Congress expects to be added to most library collections will have CIP information included on the inside of the title page or "verso" page of the item. The CIP program is a boon to librarians everywhere because it is an easily accessible source of bibliographic information and is displayed in a manner similar to a catalog record in a card catalog or OPAC (Intner &Weihs, 2015). Figure 1.2 shows CIP information for a selected title. Note that the CIP information includes the title, author, publisher, publication date, the International Standard Book Number (ISBN), subject headings, and classification numbers.

The activities of classification and cataloging in a library result in a library catalog with records that are complete and consistent, which is in contrast with information retrieved from an Internet search engine. According to Intner and Weihs (2015), standardization allows catalogs to network with each other to display contents of multiple libraries and resources in multiple formats while still providing consistency in the organization and display of information for the user.

Library of Congress Cataloging-in-Publication Data

Riedling, Ann Marlow, 1952–
    [Reference skills for the school library media specialist]
    Reference skills for the school librarian : tools and tips / Ann Marlow Riedling, Loretta Shake, and Cynthia Houston. — Third edition.
        pages cm
    Includes bibliographical references and index.
    ISBN 978-1-58683-528-6 (paperback) — ISBN 978-1-58683-529-3 (ebook)
    1. School libraries—Reference services—United States. 2. Children's reference books. 3. Children's electronic reference sources. 4. Internet in school libraries. I. Shake, Loretta. II. Houston, Cynthia. III. Title.
    Z675.S3R54   2013
    025.5'2778—dc23   2012036617

ISBN: 978-1-58683-528-6
EISBN: 978-1-58683-529-3

17 16 15 14 13   1 2 3 4 5

This book is also available on the World Wide Web as an eBook.
Visit www.abc-clio.com for details.

Linworth
An Imprint of ABC-CLIO, LLC

ABC-CLIO, LLC
130 Cremona Drive, P.O. Box 1911
Santa Barbara, California 93116-1911

This book is printed on acid-free paper ♾
Manufactured in the United States of America

Figure 1.2. Cataloging in Publication information found in books cataloged by the Library of Congress

FEATURES OF A LIBRARY CATALOG

Automated library catalogs typically contain features that have traditionally been a part of library catalogs since the 19th century. The feature that is most visible to the user is the OPAC, which can display records by title, author, subject, or keyword. Another feature of the library catalog users are not familiar with is the shelf list, which lists items as they are arranged on the shelf by classification. Librarians use the shelf list when they are checking the arrangement of books on the library shelf and searching for missing items. Also, a feature of library catalogs users rarely see is the authority file, which is a list of name and subject headings used for assigning subject headings to

```
Lewis Carroll's Alice's Adventures in Wonderland : a Documentary Volume
MARC Tags

000   02173cam a2200421 i 4500
001   18065144
005   20141112111545.0
008   140312s2014 miu b 001 0 eng
906   ____   |a 7 |b cbc |c orignew |d 1 |e ecip |f 20 |g y-gencatlg
925   0_     |a acquire |b 1 shelf copy |x policy default
               |b xk14 2014-03-12 |i xk14 2014-03-12 ONIX |w xk14 2014-03-12 to CIP |a xn12 2014-10-22 1 copy rec'd., to CIP ver. |f xk23
955   ____    2014-11-12 to CALM
010   ____   |a  2014002017
020   ____   |a 9780787696504 (hardback)
020   ____   |a 0787696501 (hardcover)
040   ____   |a DLC |b eng |c DLC |e rda |d DLC
042   ____   |a pcc
043   ____   |a e-uk-en
050   00     |a PR4611.A73  |b L55 2014
082   00     |a 823/.8  |2 23
084   ____   |a LCO002000 |a LIT004020 |a BIO007000 |2 bisacsh
               |a Lewis Carroll's Alice's Adventures in Wonderland : |b a Documentary Volume / |c edited by Carolyn Sigler, University of
245   00      Minnesota Duluth.
264   _1     |a Detroit : |b Gale, Cengage Learning, |c [2014]
300   ____   |a xxv, 466 pages : |b illustrations ; |c 29 cm.
336   ____   |a text |2 rdacontent
337   ____   |a unmediated |2 rdamedia
338   ____   |a volume |2 rdacarrier
490   0_     |a Dictionary of Literary Biography ;  |v 375
               |a "Documents on the writing, reception, and reputation of Lewis Carroll's Alice's Adventures in Wonderland"-- |c Provided
520   ____    by publisher.
               |a "This award-winning multi-volume series is dedicated to making literature and its creators better understood and more
               accessible to students and interested readers, while satisfying the standards of librarians, teachers and scholars. Dictionary of
520   ____    Literary"-- |c Provided by publisher.
504   ____   |a Includes bibliographical references and index.
600   10     |a Carroll, Lewis, |d 1832-1898. |t Alice's adventures in Wonderland.
650   _0     |a Fantasy fiction, English |x History and criticism.
650   _0     |a Children's stories, English |x History and criticism.
600   00     |a Alice |c (Fictitious character from Carroll)
650   _7     |a LITERARY COLLECTIONS / American / General. |2 bisacsh
650   _7     |a LITERARY CRITICISM / American / General. |2 bisacsh
650   _7     |a BIOGRAPHY & AUTOBIOGRAPHY / Literary. |2 bisacsh
700   1_     |a Sigler, Carolyn, |d 1958- |e editor of compilation.
```

Figure 1.3. MARC record example

items in the catalog. The authority file is used to apply subject headings to items being cataloged as part of the subject analysis process (Taylor, 2000). These different features help to keep items in the library organized in the catalog and on the library shelves so they can be easily accessed by library users.

The large wooden card catalogs are now the province of antique stores because most library records are in electronic format. Electronic catalog records allow information sharing between libraries and simplify the process of entering new records into the catalog. Figure 1.3 is an example of a catalog record in the machine-readable cataloging record (MARC) format most familiar to librarians. Note that areas for the title, author, publisher, subject heading, and call number are all found on this record. The additional numbers and letters found on the MARC record instruct the computer in how to display the record in the OPAC. Although a library record in MARC format appears to be confusing, with practice and experience, librarians have no difficulty reading, under-standing, and creating original catalog records.

THE PURPOSE OF THE LIBRARY CATALOG

People who are not familiar with the technical side of library automation or classi-fication and cataloging activities may not initially understand the importance of library catalogs in the age of Internet search engines. Simply put, the purpose of library cata-logs is to impose order on some corner of the chaotic bibliographic universe we live in and to help us find the authoritative information we need in order to live successfully in the 21st century.

As the bibliographic universe has expanded in both the physical and virtual worlds, libraries have struggled in their attempts to impose order on this chaotic information environment. While classification and cataloging technologies, standards, and proce-dures continuously change, the goals for the library catalog have always been the same since the 19th century: to organize information in the best means possible for the user.

Charles Cutter's *Rules for a Dictionary Catalog*, written in 1876, are as true for the 21st century as they were for the 19th century. According to Cutter, the function of the library catalog should be to allow the user to:

1. Find an item when the author, title, or subject is known.
2. Find what the library holdings are in relation to a given author, title, or subject.
3. Assist with the choice of an item based on the edition, format, or character of an item.

These are referred to as the Finding, Location, and Collocation functions of the catalog, which are to:

1. Finding—find an item by its known characteristics.
2. Location—assign a unique location for each item in the catalog.
3. Collocation—group like items together. (Taylor, 2004)

The purposes of classification and cataloging tasks are to further the rules and func-tions of the library catalog described by Cutter in the 19th century. In the 21st century, librarians believe that "it's all about the user"—meaning that the library catalog and the arrangement of items in the physical and virtual library worlds should meet the needs of the user, first and foremost. So, even though it might be more convenient for the librarian to have all the books reside in a locked area and retrieved by patron request, this would not further the purpose of the library catalog to meet the needs of the user. Cutter's princi-ples assert that libraries and library catalogs should be organized and presented in a man-ner that best serves the public, and when the public mind changes, so must the catalog.

LIBRARY CATALOGS AS INFORMATION DISCOVERY SYSTEMS

In the 1990s, OPACs were essentially databases of items used to organize the col-lection, link users with databases of other libraries, and aid information retrieval. These are now referred to as "legacy" or "traditional" automated catalogs. These systems typically limit search options to specific fields such as subject, author, title, or key-word in title, and results are displayed in textual form. In later years, newer automated systems, called library 2.0, added more user-friendly and visually appealing features such as the ability to display book jackets, keyword searching, and interconnections between local library holdings and larger library networks. A library 2.0 feature called federated searching allows users to use one search box for searching multiple information databases, linking users to print and electronic resources with one query (Casey, 2007). WorldCat Local is an application of the WorldCat information discovery tool for individual libraries that allows federated searching to library users who want to search multiple library catalogs and databases in a single interface from their own library.

With more and more computing power available for libraries to use, a new generation of library catalogs is now under development. Called next-generation library catalogs, these systems take advantage of the ability of the Internet to connect information portals, to analyze and display information in different ways, and to create collaborative participatory communities for sharing information. Next-generation catalogs have the potential to add social and interactive dimensions to the catalog, such as user-generated reviews and rankings. With the newer generation of library catalogs, the focus is on users' social and information needs inside and outside library. The next-generation catalogs also have the ability to enhance library public services such as readers' advisory, collection development, reference, and youth services (Tarulli & Spiteri, 2012). There are specific features of next-generation catalogs that many librarians believe have the ability to enhance users' information discovery experience (Casey, 2007; Tarulli & Spiteri, 2012). Here is a list of the most common characteristic of a next-generation library catalog.

Next-Generation Web Features

- Cloud-based information portals—the library catalog is part of the Internet information "cloud" enabling interconnectivity with other libraries and information portals.
- Platform-independent access and display—access and display of information is platform independent and can be accessed using anything that can be connected to the Internet such as a laptop, tablet, or mobile device.

User-Friendly Search Interface

- Single portal or search box—users search for information regardless of format or location using a single search box.
- Natural language searching and spell-checking—users can search for information without using special query language, and their spelling errors are automatically corrected.

Social Networking Features

- User ratings—the display of information can be ranked by relevancy, popularity, positive user reviews, and so on.
- Social networking tools—tools for online social interaction relevant to library resources such as tagging, blogs, RSS feeds, user reviews, and suggestions are embedded in the catalog.

Full Resources Available

- Full text or media—resources are available electronically in full text or audio-visual format.

Customization and Flexibility to Meet Local Needs

- Integration with local databases—the catalog program has the ability to integrate local library digital holdings, such as digital archives and genealogical information into the system.

Next-generation library catalogs are coming closer to meeting users' expectations of a user-friendly information discovery tool similar to what they experience when using Internet search engines, but because users expect high-quality resources to be retrieved from an OPAC search, libraries face some challenges with how they handle the multiplicity of information resources and formats they can deliver. Some libraries have separate areas in the catalog for searching print materials, audiovisual collections, eBooks, websites, and periodical databases. Other libraries allow users to search for different types of information all at once via what is referred to as a "federated" search. Some believe that when information resources are organized into different areas that users must search separately, a barrier to information access is created, called an information "silo." However, others believe that when disparate information resources are aggregated and can be searched at once, the amount of information to be maintained and managed becomes unwieldy and diminishes the quality of the catalog (Barton & Mak, 2012).

UNIQUE FEATURES OF SCHOOL LIBRARY CATALOGS

To date, not one library automation solution offers all the features of a next-generation catalog. However, we know that children and young adults are attracted to many of these next-generation features, particularly any feature of a catalog that presents information visually or assists them with the vocabulary or spelling tasks they might not feel confident with during the search process. Users of school library catalogs are often young children who are preliterate, may not speak English as the first language, or may not be sophisticated searchers. Because of the specific needs of their users, automated catalogs for school libraries should be tailored to meet the needs and interests of a school-age population (Druin, 2005).

A substantial amount of research has been done related to how children use library catalogs to search for information. In general, school-age children's information-seeking experiences benefit when library catalogs have an easy-to-use search interface with spell-check and "did you mean" features. They also benefit from alternative ways to search for information, such as general categories, locations, and visual information displays (Hutchinson et al., 2005).

In 2002, the International Children's Digital Library (ICDL) project was launched to develop a vast online collection of international children's literature accessible by an interface designed specifically for children. Many of the features integrated into the ICDL were developed based on how children search for information. For example,

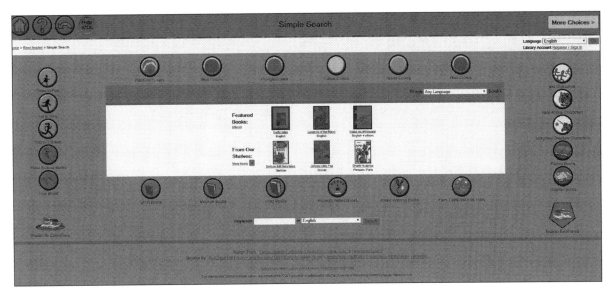

Figure 1.4. International Children's Digital Library search interface

because young children lack refined motor skills and have difficulty using a mouse, the ICDL interface uses large graphical buttons so that children can browse for information by category with one click of a mouse or touch on the screen. Children also have difficulty with using vocabulary to search for information. For this reason, the ICDL created child-centered categories so that they could find titles related to color, feeling, subject, and genre. Figure 1.4 shows the ICDL search interface and some of the unique features that have been designed for children in mind (Hutchinson et al., 2005).

Destiny Quest developed by the Follett Corporation is an automated library catalog designed specifically for school libraries. The system does contain many of the features of child-friendly and next-generation search interfaces including visually interesting displays, natural language searching, and social networking options.

Library catalogs have changed dramatically since their inception in the early centuries. Once, catalogs were simply lists of items in the collection. Now many catalogs are complex networked portals to electronic and print resources in the physical and virtual worlds. The concepts, rules, and procedures used to organize information for library catalogs are part of classification and cataloging activities and involve description, subject analysis, classification, and assigning a call number. The overarching goal of classification and cataloging is to create a standardized, user-friendly display for library catalogs and further Cutter's function of the library catalog so that resources are made readily available to the user.

DISCUSSION QUESTIONS

1. Select a library catalog to evaluate. Have the librarian explain the features and function of the catalog and ask about its positive and negative attributes. Go to the website of the selected system and review the features it advertises.

List information about the general features and any reviews about how well it serves the library users. Describe how easy or difficult the catalog is to search for items.

2. Select an online catalog to evaluate such as a public or academic library catalog, the Library of Congress catalog, or any other available information discovery tool such as WorldCat. Determine what aspects of next-generation systems the catalog exhibits.

2

The Automated School Library

INTRODUCTION

"Oh, dear," said Ms. Huss, the school librarian, "little Joanie still has that copy of the *Spaceflight Manual* on her tablet, and Timmy has been wanting to read it for weeks." Ms. Huss speaks into her discreetly placed earbud, "Leslie, could you send Joanie Pappas a text, asking her to return her copy of *Spaceflight Manual*?" The screen on her tablet illuminates a picture of a cartoon avatar called "Leslie," the school library automation system, who is sporting glasses, bun, sensible shoes, and cardigan. Leslie responds, "Ms. Huss, I sent Joanie a text last week, and she responded that she would return the eBook tomorrow." Ms. Huss responded gratefully, "Thanks again, Leslie, you are really on top of things. What would I do without you?"

Although this scenario sounds a bit futuristic, the next-generation automated school library systems will have capabilities to manage routine library activities on a level we can hardly imagine and will become increasingly important tools for supporting school librarians' roles as information specialists and instructional partners.

INTEGRATED LIBRARY SYSTEMS

The school library automation system, often referred to as the "Integrated Library System" or ILS, is an essential organizing tool for all of the physical and virtual library collections. The ILS comprises different features or "modules" that assist the school librarian with all of the collection management activities in the library, including selecting and deleting resources, creating and maintaining catalog records, circulation of materials, creating and maintaining patron records, and promoting library services such as curriculum alignment, readers' advisory, and student book clubs. In essence, the ILS is the technology heart of the library, and its health and well-being is a key responsibility for the school librarian.

School librarians typically manage small collections within a district-wide unit. These collections are developed to meet the information needs of the school-age population using the library. For these reasons, the automation needs of a school library are different from the needs of public, academic, and special libraries. The capabilities of the ILS really determines the types of information students will be able to locate and access, the ease with which they can access both physical and virtual materials, and the effort school librarians make to manage these materials and engage students in information inquiry activities.

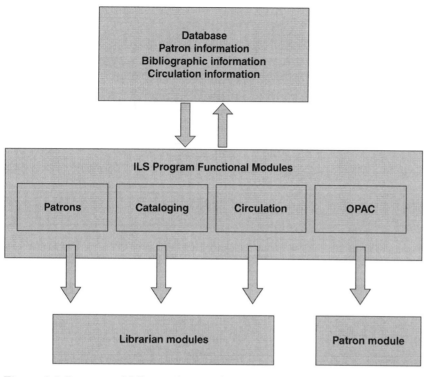

Figure 2.1. Integrated Library System functions

Depending on its capabilities, a school library's ILS can manage all the functions of a media center, including the library catalog, circulation of materials, collection analysis, managing user accounts, conducting library inventories, library materials promotion, and reporting. Essentially, a library automation system is an information system that integrates different databases for managing the functions of the library. Figure 2.1 illustrates how an ILS functions to manage the information databases used in different activities of a library.

Notice how all the functions of the library such as circulation and cataloging use the same database to retrieve information. This is because all the components of an ILS are interdependent. For example, when a new item is added to the library, it is added to the library catalog database. In order to see whether the library has that item, a user consults the OPAC, which queries the catalog database to see whether the item exists. In order to determine whether the book is available, information from the database is queried using the circulation module and is displayed in the OPAC.

Because library automation has taken over many of the routine tasks performed by the school librarians, the implementation of the ILS in school media centers has dramatically changed the role of the school librarian from the "keeper of the books" to information technology specialist and learning commons manager.

Characteristics of Library Automation Systems

There are a number of different library automation systems available for school libraries to use. The basic functions and features of these systems are very similar. What distinguishes these systems from each other is the level to which next-generation features have been integrated into the different components of the system. For example, all library OPACs display information about an item in the library and its availability; however, some OPACs have the capability to display not only information about the item, but a picture of the book jacket, links to reviews, and similar items in different formats as well.

All automation systems rely on computer hardware, program software, and networking technology to function, but again, the types of hardware, software, and networks these systems use determine the extent to which next-generation features of library catalogs are feasible.

The library automation systems found in school libraries today range from state-of-the-art cloud-based systems to what are called legacy systems. The older legacy systems use an information database housed either on a stand-alone computer in the school library or on a network-based file server in a school district technology center. In both these cases, the library hardware, software, and records are managed locally, and access to wider information about holdings in other libraries via the library OPAC is limited. By contrast, more recent cloud-based computing technology allows educational institutions to store and access library records on the Internet. In this case, the hardware and Internet access are managed locally, while the software and information databases are managed through the ILS vendor as a subscription service. The trend toward cloud-based subscription library automation services is termed the Software-as-a-service model and offers small and large school libraries with the opportunity to use a sophisticated automation system without extensive investment in networking equipment and licensing (Breeding, 2014).

A number of library automation systems use what is called open-source technology, which refers to the programming code available free for programmers to create anything they want, including an ILS. Open-source programming frees libraries from dependence on library automation software licensing and subscription fees. The use of open-source software programs relies on having skilled programmers available to customize and maintain the program. There are strengths and weaknesses associated with open-source technology, because it requires skilled information technology staff to maintain.

Desirable Features of Library Automation Systems

According to automation systems expert Marshall Breeding (2014), the basic features of a library automation system for school libraries should provide flexibility and interoperability. In other words, the features of the ILS should be flexible in their design, easily adaptable to district and school requirements, allow the systems to work well with other student information systems used in the district, and support use from tablets and other mobile devices. In general, school library automation systems should have the following capabilities:

- Interoperability with student information systems—student records from existing student information systems should be easily integrated into the patron records system of the ILS so that student library records contain grade-level, classroom, reading-level, special needs, and other student information useful to the librarian.
- Interoperability with eBook and periodical database providers—eBooks from outside vendors, online resources from periodical database providers, and selected websites should be easily integrated into the library catalog and be available in full text format so that students can access resources inside and outside the library.
- Interoperability with local and state-level public libraries and library resource providers—resources offered by public libraries or state-level library resources should be easily integrated into the ILS so that students may access materials from a larger library network.

- Flexibility in migrating and upgrading catalog records—school libraries do not have extensive cataloging personnel to create and maintain catalog records, so the ILS should be able to access and download catalog records and minimize the task of editing and managing records at the local level.
- Flexibility for meeting local information management needs—the ILS should be designed to accommodate local needs to manage other school resources such as technology equipment and textbooks.
- Flexibility for supporting current and emerging technologies—the ILS should be accessible from current technologies such as tablets and mobile devices and be designed to accommodate emerging technologies.

Most automated systems for school libraries have some but not all of these capabilities. For example, most systems have the ability to import catalog records from different sources, but some systems have made this process more streamlined than others. Some systems do provide a means for student information to be downloaded from a district or state student information database, while other systems may not have this capability. Many but not all school ILSs have applications or apps so that the catalog can be accessed on tablets and mobile devices.

Automated Library Systems: Functional Modules

Although the basic features of automated library systems including the hardware, software, and networking technology may differ, the basic functions of the ILS are very similar. All of these systems were developed to provide different programs or functional modules to manage the activities of a library. According to Bilal (2014), the following modules are essential components of a library automation system:

- Library catalog—the library catalog is a database and program used to create, store, retrieve, and manage bibliographic records. The library user sees only the OPAC component of this module when they search for items stored in the library catalog database. The OPAC and Catalog modules work together to maintain and display library records.
- Circulation management—this module is used by library staff for managing the lending, return, renewal, holds of library materials, and user fines and fees for lost items. Circulation management modules include a database of library users or patrons, which contain their personal information and library privileges. This module may or may not store historic information about specific books patrons have borrowed, as many librarians believe this is a violation of library users' right to privacy.
- Acquisitions—the acquisitions module is used for ordering, receiving, and paying for library materials from library vendors.
- Serials—not always found in a school library ILS, this module manages serials the library holds such as magazines and journals. This modules manages ordering, payment, and inventory of serial publications in the library.
- Reporting—the reports module of an ILS compiles library statistics about circulation, use of the collection, and is used for strategic analysis and review of

library operations. An essential feature is the inventory program that works with the catalog and circulation modules to maintain a shelf list of items that can be checked when the library is taking an inventory of its holdings. The inventory activities account for missing or incorrectly shelved items.

- Authority control—this module uses the catalog database to maintain the consistency of headings used in describing bibliographic materials. This module enables libraries to develop a list of locally relevant subject and name headings for their records. This feature is important to school libraries because it enables them to maintain a consistent list of developmentally appropriate subject headings for their users.

- Library services—typically part of a next-generation catalog, this module integrates different social networking applications such as blogs, RSS feeds, Pinterest, or Twitter feeds into the ILS in order to promote library services such as reference and readers' advisory.

Figure 2.2 shows a display of the different modules that are a part of an ILS. Along the top right side of the screen, you will see icons for the Catalog, Patrons, Circulation, Serials, Inventory, Reports, Settings, and OPAC modules. This is an example of how an ILS provides access to the different functional modules used to manage library activities.

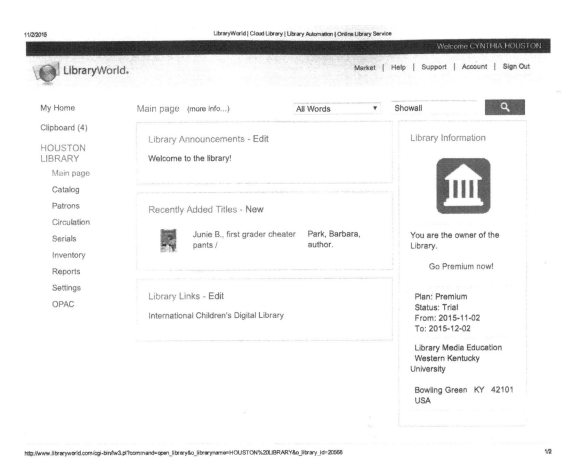

Figure 2.2. ILS functional modules

Automated Library Systems: Next-Generation Features

In recent years, automated library systems have included a variety of social networking features in their catalogs with the goal of integrating user participation into the OPAC and enhancing the overall appeal of the catalog as an information discovery tool. Referred to as next-generation features, these social networking tools primarily impact the catalog module of an ILS as these features allow users to add information to the catalog record such as a subject tag or user review. Figure 2.3 shows how next-generation features such as a picture of the book jacket, links to other works, reader reviews, and keyword tags have been incorporated into the OPAC.

In 2007, school librarians weighed in with their opinions on which features of a next-generation catalog was of most interest to them (Fiehn, 2007). The survey indicated that the most desired features were those that helped students access books in their area of interest, aided in collection development, and facilitated communication between the librarian and the students. The top next-generation features of most interest to school librarians include the following:

- Top 10 books notes
- New Arrivals notes
- Links to similar items for reader's advisory
- Student reviews

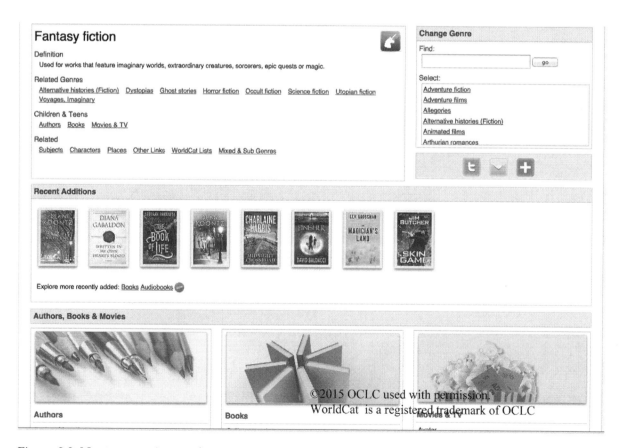

Figure 2.3. Next-generation catalog

- Wish lists and purchase recommendations
- Digital content such as eBooks and eZines
- Patron-to-patron communication (Fiehn, 2007)

Discovery Interfaces

The library catalog is the most visible component of the ILS and, in concert with a well-designed library website, connects students with all the items they may need for their personal and academic uses. In an information silo environment, information is separated into different areas of the library information portal in different applications such as digital archives, OPACs, periodical databases, and eBooks. Student research activities in an information silo would use more than one source to locate information in different formats. For example, students would use the OPAC to locate physical materials such as books, DVDs, or CDs; the online periodical database to access magazine and journal articles in electronic format; and an Internet search engine to locate websites.

With the advent of library discovery interfaces and services, students do not have to search for information in different information silos. A discovery interface works with the ILS to bring together all the different databases students can use to search for information into one search box. With one query, students can find information in different sources such as multiple library holdings, periodical databases, and authoritative websites. Discovery services are a cloud-based version of the discovery interface and makes wider search for information possible via the world of eBooks, journals, newspapers, and digital archives located on the Internet cloud. According to Bilal (2014), the discovery interface is actually a form of a next-generation library catalog in that it is a cloud-based application allowing a user to search multiple information sources with one search query—features that bring us closer to the ideal library catalog.

LIBRARY AUTOMATION SYSTEMS: STANDARDS

Automated library systems are able to access records from other libraries because standardization in the format and structure of library records and network communication protocols allow seamless interconnections between library databases. Two key standardized features of library automation systems that enable interconnectivity are the MARC record and the Z39.50 standard. MARC format is the standard used for creating catalog records that computers can see and display in a consistent format in the library OPAC. The Z39 network standard enables automation systems to connect and exchange information. Both of these standards were developed and are maintained by the Library of Congress.

Network Standards

In order for libraries to make their information available online and connect with other libraries, standards are necessary for their computers to be able to communicate. The Z39.50 standard refers to the International Standard, ISO 23950, *Information Retrieval (Z39.50): Application Service Definition and Protocol Specification*, ANSI/NISO Z39.50. This standard enables users to search and retrieve catalog records from multiple library databases from remote locations. The Z39.50 software is available free from a site maintained by the Library of Congress (Taylor, 2000).

Standards for Bibliographic Records

Machine-Readable Catalog Record (MARC) and BIBFRAME

The MARC format is the standard for computer library records across the globe. The different tags, fields, and indicators in a MARC record instruct the computer to display information in a particular way in the OPAC. It also enables specific fields in the OPAC to be searched in order to retrieve specific information for the user. Finally, the MARC format instructs the OPAC how to display lists of results of a search in a consistent manner. Because vendors of library automation systems support standardization and the MARC format, libraries can migrate or transfer data from one ILS to another. Because the MARC record is an international standard, library records from other states and countries can be exchanged, enabling users to search different OPACs and see their results displayed in a consistent manner. The most current MARC standard is MARC21, but the Library of Congress is working on a new standard for automated catalog records called BIBFRAME, which will provide records more compatible with relational databases now being used in automated catalog systems (Bibliographic Framework Initiative, 2015).

Resource Description and Access (RDA)

The RDA cataloging standards were designed to move descriptive cataloging into the 21st century. For example, RDA standards have more terms for describing materials in different formats, so that DVDs, CDs, and websites can all be described in the library catalog. As another example, the relational database computer programming that underlies the RDA concept now enables different expressions of a work, such as Shakespeare's *Romeo and Juliet*, to be connected to each other in the catalog. In a 21st-century catalog, users are able to look up the play *Romeo and Juliet* and be connected to movies, websites, and graphic novels, all based on the original work by Shakespeare. Figure 2.4 of a library OPAC shows how the concepts behind RDA are integrated into an automated catalog, consequently providing a greater variety of descriptions for items and connections between similar works. As the RDA standards are implemented, these features will be increasingly more evident in both the cataloging and OPAC modules of ILSs (Sullivan, 2013).

SCHOOL LIBRARY AUTOMATION SYSTEMS

In the United States, 88 percent of the 79,000 school libraries in public schools use automated catalogs, making it a very strong market for this type of information system. Today, there are several automated library systems tailored to meet the needs of the modern school library (National Center for Educational Statistics, 2013). The proceeding list does not exhaust the automated systems available for school libraries, but does provide examples of different formats and technologies applied to library automation systems.

Follett Destiny

By far, the most popular ILS is Follett Destiny by Follett School Solutions. Follett is a well-known business in education as it is the main provider of print and electronic

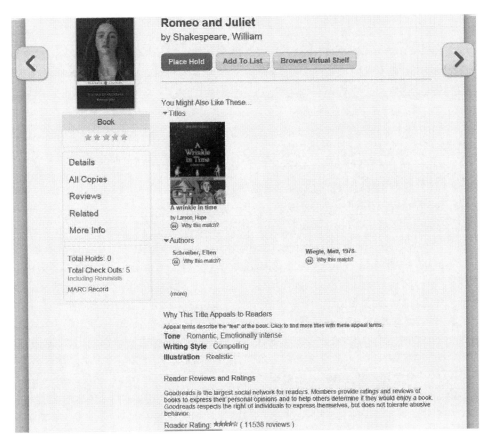

Figure 2.4. Sample OPAC Record with RDA Concepts

educational resources to schools and school libraries. The Follett Destiny Library Manager is used by more than half of the schools in the United States (Breeding, 2014). The Destiny Library Manager is one of the leading-edge ILS applications for school libraries on the market. In 2013, the system was updated to support new cataloging standards and mobile applications, and to improve reporting and acquisitions modules. The providers have also improved the integration of print and electronic holdings into the catalog (Breeding, 2014).

Atrium

A much smaller portion of school libraries use the Atrium ILS, from Book Systems, Inc. This ILS is a web-based application with features that allow integration of eBooks from Overdrive—a large provider of eBooks to school and public libraries—and new applications for mobile devices. Atrium also offers a developmentally appropriate graphical search interface for the Pre-K through third-grade library user.

OPALS

OPALS developed by Media Flex, Inc., is an open-source ILS used in K-12 settings, most notably in New York State. Media Flex provides hosting services for the OPALS system, and there is no subscription fee associated with the software.

Library World

Library World is a web-based ILS with more than 3,000 users including more than 200 school libraries. In Library World, all the functions of a library management system are cloud based and are conducted via the Internet, with information stored at a remote location.

MANAGING AND MAINTAINING SCHOOL LIBRARY AUTOMATION SYSTEMS

The high-tech nature of managing and maintaining the school library automation system has made mastery of technology skills essential for a librarian's effectiveness in the school. As technology changes, the standards for cataloging information also change. As part of a school or district leadership team, the school librarian is an active participant on any decision-making committee for upgrading or purchasing an automated library system. As a team member, the school librarian is involved in reviewing different systems and examining how well the components integrate with each other, how effective the management system serves the functions of the library, and how the OPAC helps students to locate, access, and use library materials. Regular maintenance of the ILS such as updating catalog and patron records is part and parcel of using an automated library catalog. In addition, continuous training for staff and students on how best to use the features of the ILS is an important part of a school librarians' job as an information specialist.

AUTOMATION SYSTEMS AND STUDENT LEARNING

The automated school library catalog, which is now available to many students at home and on their mobile devices, has the potential to support student learning in a variety of ways. Library catalogs provide students with access to materials in a variety of formats. In this way, an ILS enhances student access to a wide variety of resources. Library catalogs as an information discovery tool can support students in their efforts to be effective users of information and ideas because it plays an important role in the information inquiry process via vocabulary development and in learning information-seeking strategies. School librarians recognize that the library catalog is an instructional tool and work with students to develop the vocabulary and metacognitive skills for effective information inquiry.

DISCUSSION QUESTIONS

1. Use websites and articles about two ILSs for school libraries and compare and contrast their modules and features.
2. Select a next-generation library catalog to evaluate. Based on information from this chapter, discuss how next-generation features are used to promote use of library resources and services.
3. Discuss ideas for how library catalogs can be used to support student learning based on national curriculum standards.

4. Given the high-tech and ubiquitous nature of many school library catalogs, discuss how children's access to technology at home might impact their ability to take advantage of this information resource.
5. Take time to observe young children use the library catalog in a school or public library. Note which type of OPAC is used, whether the interface is geared toward young children, and the successes and frustrations they experience when searching for information. Based on this information, think of some ideas for how library OPACs might be designed for preliterate, early readers, and English language learners.

3

Standards for Organizing the Bibliographic Universe

INTRODUCTION

Once upon a time, a middle-grade student was looking for a copy of one of her favorite books, *The Little Prince* by Antoine de Saint-Exupéry. She decided to use World-Cat to search for the title because she wanted to see all the versions of the work that were available. The student typed in the title and retrieved the vast world of *The Little Prince* contained in libraries all over the globe. She explored holdings related to the title in the National Library of France and also the Library of Congress (LC). Moving seamlessly from one source to another, she found books, movies, animated cartoons, exhibitions, websites, and literary criticism related to the work. She was amazed to find that even her local library held different versions of the book as well as audiobooks and animated video adaptations.

The story of a student's search for *The Little Prince* is an example of how library users are able to move easily from one library OPAC to another without any major differences between the ways in which records are displayed. Several organizations carry the bulk of the responsibility for maintaining cataloging standards. These organizations cooperate to develop rules and standards for cataloging materials from all over the world in a multiplicity of languages.

NATIONAL AND INTERNATIONAL ORGANIZATIONS

The International Federation of Library Associations (IFLA)

As the world becomes increasingly interconnected through the World Wide Web, the need for libraries across the world to follow standard classification and cataloging practices is critical. For this reason, the International Federation of Library Associations (IFLA) in coordination with national libraries across the globe currently set the cataloging standards followed by all members of the organization regardless of language or country. IFLA is the international body comprising individual and institutional members of school, public, private, and academic libraries across the globe. As an organization, it represents the interests of library and information service providers and their users. Essentially, IFLA is the global voice of the library and information profession. As a governing body, IFLA establishes and maintains standards for best practices, conceptual models for bibliographic and authority data, digital format codes, rules for describing resources, and a number of different guidelines for libraries and services to the public (Current IFLA Standards, 2014). These standards are reviewed internationally and updated regularly by the organization. Standards relevant to cataloging established by IFLA include Functional Requirements for Bibliographic Records (FRBR), Functional Requirements for Authority Data (FRAD), the Statement on International Cataloging Principals (ICP), and International Standards for Bibliographic Description (ISBD). Together, the standards specify how catalog records are to be formatted, described, and prepared for retrieval and display in an automated environment. These international rules and procedures are responsible for making online library catalogs across the world easy to search and access using a variety of information discovery tools.

The American Library Association (ALA)

The American Library Association (ALA) is the national professional association representing information service workers employed in all types of organizations in the United States and internationally. As a governing body, the ALA issues policies, standards, and guidelines to help members improve library services to patrons. The Association for Library Collections and Technical Services, a division of ALA, provides guidelines, technical support, and professional development for the cataloging community and is a member of the steering committee for establishing and maintaining international cataloging rules such as the AACR and RDA. The ALA develops and distributes important publications for the classification and cataloging world such as the RDA cataloging standards in print and online formats (ALA, 2015).

Library of Congress (LC)

Much of the standards and practices for cataloging and classification originated in the Library of Congress, which, because it is the depository for copyrighted materials, is one of the world's largest libraries. The LC is not only the official library for the legislative branches of government, but also the depository for important documents that are part of American history and culture. To maintain consistency in its own records, the LC created standard cataloging procedures and its own classification systems. As the number of libraries grew across the nation, other libraries adopted classification and cataloging practices begun in the LC. For years, the LC supplied catalog cards for libraries to purchase so they did not have to create records themselves.

When library catalogs became automated, the LC supplied electronic records, referred to as MARC records. As a member of the steering committee on cataloging standards, the LC continues to coordinate the national and international committees overseeing classification and cataloging practices across the globe. Currently, the LC is working with other organizations and institutions to establish and support the new RDA cataloging standards ("About OCLC," 2015).

Online Computer Library Center (OCLC)

The OCLC is a nonprofit consortium comprising all types of libraries in 113 countries who work together to develop, organize, and share information resources in an online environment. The consortium serves an organizing and coordinating function for creating and sharing catalog records that meet international and national standards and provides a centralized resource for members to create and obtain quality catalog records. Some important cataloging tools and services provided by OCLC include contract cataloging services, subscription services for creating and sharing online catalog records, DDC tools, and WorldCat information discovery services. Because of the vast number of records held by the OCLC and the services they provide, most academic and public libraries are members of this consortium. An important information discovery tool available to the public from OCLC is WorldCat, the world's largest online public access catalog, and WorldCat Local, a version of WorldCat designed for use by individual libraries. WorldCat and WorldCat Local connect local libraries to library holdings at the regional, state, national, and international levels (OCLC, 2015).

RULES AND FORMATS GOVERNING CATALOG RECORDS

The international organizations discussed in the previous section oversee the development of the rules governing how catalog records are conceptualized and created. The rules all function to make catalog records as accessible to the user as possible. The current standards for library catalogs, FRBR, FRAD, and RDA, were developed not only to link users with specific items related to their search, but also to link users to related items, the creators of those items, their relationships, and items available from a number of providers. The rules are founded in the following four key tasks a user engages in when searching for information and further Cutter's principles for the library catalog:

- To find a work—use data to find materials that correspond to the user's stated search criteria.
- To identify an expression—use the data retrieved to identify an entity.
- To select a manifestation—use the data to select an entity that is appropriate to the user's needs.
- To obtain an item—use the data in order to acquire or obtain access to the entity described. (Functional Requirements for Bibliographic Records, 2009)

The idea behind the cataloging standards is to develop international specifications for how an automated library catalog as a type of information database should function to match the user with information. In the past, one catalog record contained everything a librarian needed on an item for a local catalog in one table of information. When a user looks for information with an OPAC, the database system searches all of the record tables it contains and retrieves a list of relevant results. This is what is called a flat file database system. Newer database programs use a relational database design in which different areas of information are contained in different tables in different locations, all of which are linked to each other through specified relationships. This means that all of the information in a catalog record is no longer contained in one file, but because the program searches a number of different information sources, a much richer trove of data can be retrieved by a user when they are searching for information (Barton & Mak, 2012).

When a user looks for information, typically, they are searching for contents regardless of format and would like to see a wide range of information connected to

Table 3.1
Comparison of the Flat File and Relational Databases

	Organization of Information	User Experience	Example
Flat file database	Single database organizes data into fields contained in one record table	OPAC search retrieves records related to users' search of records in a single database	School library catalog search retrieves one book and one audiobook, with location and availability information
Relational database	Multiple databases organizes data into fields contained in multiple records that are interlinked with other databases	OPAC search retrieves records related to users' term and related links to other records from multiple databases	Amazon.com search retrieves 36,093 results from books to T-shirts available from Amazon and other sources, plus related items by author or genre

what they are looking for. After defining a narrower idea of what they are interested in, users will select a specific piece of information to look at in more detail and examine that item as well as related information. Many library catalogs are very limited in their ability to search and display information with any richness in format or describe their relations to other pieces of information. This is because the database programs used in these library catalogs follow a set of cataloging standards designed for the flat file format. When comparing findings from a search of the Amazon catalog of items for sale with a library catalog, it is easy to see the differences between the flat and relational database structure. Table 3.1 summarizes the similarities and differences between the flat file and relational database file structures in relation to the library catalog.

Functional Requirements for Bibliographic Records (FRBR)

Because users want their information search experiences in libraries to mirror what they are experiencing on the Internet, the cataloging community has completely overhauled how information is structured and organized by developing FRBR. The new rules and procedures for catalog records have been created for library catalogs to remain a viable and relevant information discovery tool. The *FRBR* was published in 1998 by IFLA and reflects the need for the 21st-century library catalogs to not only retrieve items related to a user's search, but also link to different editions, formats, adaptations, and other variations of the item the user might also be interested in (Functional Requirements for Bibliographic Records, 2009). In its current version, FRBR describes a conceptual model and framework for how catalog records can be organized and constructed for a relational database program environment. In this type of conceptual framework, there is a catalog record for every intellectual expression and creator in the bibliographic universe. For each, different elements of the catalog record contain information organized into "entities," "attributes," and "relationships." Information about a particular intellectual work or creation is organized into the following three groups of entities all of which have unique attributes:

- Group 1 Entities—resources or intellectual expressions
- Group 2 Entities—beings or persons related to the intellectual expressions
- Group 3 Entities—subjects related to the intellectual expressions

The groups of entities are linked through their interconnected relationships with each other (Jacox, Margaret, Moll, Nimsakont, & Routt, 2014). Figure 3.1 illustrates how entities, attributes, and relationships are connected in the FRBR conceptual model.

The individual boxes represent the three groups of entities and their attributes. The arrows show that each of these groups is connected to each other via a relationship such as a subject or ownership. This diagram is indeed complicated but expresses the fact that we live in an interconnected world of rich and complex information, which can be searched and displayed using the library catalog.

Library catalogs structured using the FRBR model allow users to query entities, attributes, and relationships in a catalog record. In this way, a library catalog can display information the user is looking for and also links to related information. The FRBR model underpins the type of relational database characteristics of next-generation catalogs and is designed to move catalogs from information silos of local holdings into discovery search engines accessing a wider bibliographic universe.

The FRBR model is hierarchical, connecting entities and attributes through their relationships to each other. The Group 1 Entities contain information about the intellectual or artistic products described by name or in bibliographic descriptions. Following the FRBR concept, each work is an abstract concept, but one that is related to all the different items that are related to this concept, such as plays, movies, websites, adaptations, and fan literature. The FRBR model uses a hierarchy of work, expression, manifestation, and item to organize and connect all of the different variations of a work (Functional Requirements for Bibliographic Records, 2009).

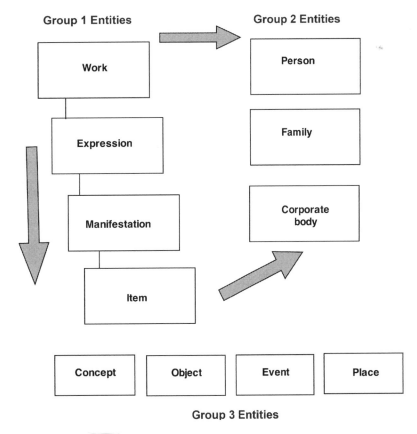

Figure 3.1. FRBR Entity relationship diagram

As an example, let's consider an intellectual endeavor we know as *Romeo and Juliet*. Because there are so many intellectual and artistic products related to *Romeo and Juliet*, we consider it a work. This is the first level of the hierarchy for a catalog record. The next level is an expression of the work. Using our example of *Romeo and Juliet* in the FRBR hierarchy, the work of *Romeo and Juliet* is at the top; below this are different expressions of the work, such as a French or German translation of Shakespeare's play; below this are different manifestations of the work such as a specific sound recording of a French translation, or a specific eBook publication of a German translation. Finally, items are the specific things the cataloger is adding to the catalog, such as the CD, on which there is the specific audio recording of the French translation, or the. pdf version of the eBook publication of the German translation. Table 3.2 describes the FRBR model related to our example.

Using the FRBR concept for a catalog, a user can search for *Romeo and Juliet* and retrieve items in different formats as well as related items in one query. According to Welsh and Bately (2012), this feature furthers Cutter's "colocation" function of the library catalog. In a catalog that uses the FRBR model, information at the work and expression levels will be available to the cataloger from a vendor or cataloging consortium. The CIP information provides information at the manifestation level. Ideally, the only information a cataloger adds to their local records at the item level would be local information such as local call number, barcode number, local subject headings, and curriculum information (Welsh & Bately, 2012).

Resources Description and Access (RDA)

RDA is the latest standard for cataloging library materials. RDA replaces AACR2R as a cataloging standard. The intent is to expand the range of materials that can be included in a library catalog to electronic and cloud-based items. RDA is an application of the FRBR conceptual model for bibliographic records and is designed to match the type of

Table 3.2
FRBR Model

FRBR Model Hierarchy and Examples		
Work—intellectual construct	*Romeo and Juliet, William Shakespeare*	
Expression—realization of the work	French Translation of Shakespeare's *Romeo and Juliet*	*Romeo and Juliet* 2013 Broadway Play starring Orlando Bloom
Manifestation—different formats of the expression	French translation of Shakespeare's *Romeo and Juliette* by Francois Pierre Guillaume Guizot published in 1864	*Romeo and Juliet* 2013 Broadway Play Script
Item—specific version of the item in a specific location	French translation of Shakespeare's *Romeo and Juliette* by Francois Pierre Guillaume Guizot published in 1864, copy in the National Library of France	*Romeo and Juliet* 2013 Broadway Play Script, copy in the New York Public Library

relational database technology used in next-generation catalogs and information discovery interfaces. The LC and the British Library began using RDA rules in 2013 so recent titles are cataloged following these guidelines. In 2013, Follett Corporation, a major vendor to school libraries, began offering records using RDA to its customers. This event signifies the wide adoption of the RDA standard in school libraries in the United States.

In RDA, there are 37 chapters governing how bibliographic records are described. The full set of RDA rules is available online from the ALA in a resource called the RDA Toolkit. There are 10 core elements that catalogers using RDA must include in their records, which are based on user tasks of finding, identifying, selecting, and obtaining items related to their information needs. Rules within each element provide guidelines for how to enter information from each of these areas into the catalog record. The RDA Appendices provide instructions on capitalization, abbreviations, relationship designators, and other details relevant to descriptive cataloging. The following elements are listed as core or required elements in records using the RDA standard:

- Title (2.3.2)
- Statement of Responsibility (2.4.2)
- Edition statement (2.5.2)
- Publication or Production information (2.8–2.12)
- Series statement (2.6)
- Identifying number (2.15)
- Mode of issuance (2.13)
- Identifying number (2.15)
- Carrier information (3.2–3.5)
- Access information (4.5–4.6) (Jacox et al., 2014)

Figure 3.2 is an example of a catalog record display based on RDA guidelines. Note that all required RDA core elements are displayed in the record. You will find that Mode of Issuance is not displayed in the record, but it is contained in the computer record.

Machine-Readable Catalog Records (MARC)

The MARC record, an acronym for machine-readable catalog record, is the standard and format used for creating database records for items entered into the automated catalog. Essentially, a MARC record is a table formatted for use by a flat file database program. The current international MARC standard is MARC21 and combines standards used in Europe, the United Kingdom, and Canada. Because MARC21 is an international standard, catalog records from around the world can be shared and displayed using different information discovery tools. The MARC standard governs the format of a MARC record, which has three parts:

- Record leader—computer code providing instructions for the computer program in how to display the catalog record.
- Directory—information for the computer program on the length, starting points, and tags for catalog records.
- Fields—the place for entering catalog information.

Below the surface / (Book)

Control Number : 2

Control Number Identifier : OCoLC

Modification Date Time : 20151102153008.0

Fixed Length Data - Additional : m o d

Physical Description - General : cr cnu|||unuuu

Fixed Length Data - General : 140313s2014 miu jo 000 1 eng d

ISBN : 9780310735021 (electronic bk.)

ISBN : 0310735025 (electronic bk.)

System Control Number : (OCoLC)872549228

Cataloging Source : TEFOD eng rda pn TEFOD TEFOD OHIOD

Library of Congress Call No : PZ7.S558625

DDCN : [Fic] 23

Main Entry-Personal Name : Shoemaker, Tim, author.

Title Statement : Below the surface / Tim Shoemaker.

Publication Distribution Data : Grand Rapids, Michigan : Zonderkidz, [2014]

Publication Distribution Data : 2014.

Physical Description : 1 online resource.

Content Type : text txt rdacontent.

Media Type : computer c rdamedia.

Carrier Type : online resource cr rdacarrier.

Series Statement : Code of silence novel.

Summary Note : Something is wrong with Cooper. He's plagued by a fear he doesn't understand and can't control. Is there really a body floating in the underwater currents of the lake?.

588 : Description based on print version record.

Subject-Topical Term : Fear Juvenile fiction.

Subject-Topical Term : Friendship Juvenile fiction.

Subject-Topical Term : Witnesses Juvenile fiction.

Subject-Topical Term : Conduct of life Juvenile fiction.

Index Term-Genre/Form : Electronic books.

Figure 3.2. Catalog record following RDA standard

The leader and directory parts of the MARC record provide information for the computer program used for searching and displaying the records. Because the first two parts of a MARC record are basically computer code, a librarian deals primarily with the field area of the MARC record. Each MARC field comprises a three-digit tag that denotes a different piece of bibliographic information such as the author's name, title, publication information, or description. Each MARC tag also has a two-digit indicator, which provides additional information about specific aspects of that particular tag, and subfield codes, which identify different parts of the information being entered in the field. For example, one indicator may specify that the first word of the title is to be ignored by a search engine because the words are "a," "and," or "the," or a subfield code may indicate that the information describes the date or language of a work. In most catalogs, subfield codes are preceded by a pipe-mark | or a dollar sign $. Most school library automated cataloging systems provide sufficient guidance so that catalogers do not have to be able to recall specific indicators and subfield codes for their items. The MARC record in Figure 3.3 shows examples of different parts of the MARC record and the location of the tags, indicators, and subfields in a MARC21 record (Furrie, 2009).

The most common MARC fields mirror the required bibliographic areas specified by RDA, including the author, title, publication, and physical description areas.

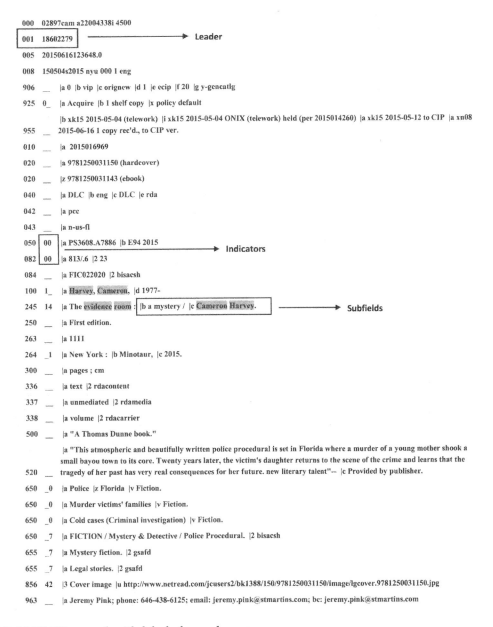

Figure 3.3. MARC21 record with labels for each area

Table 3.3 shows the areas of description required by international standards and the associated MARC21 tag.

Because the MARC record is designed for a flat file database program, a new standard for catalog records called Bibframe is being developed. According to the LC, the entity overseeing the development of the new standard:

> The BIBFRAME Initiative is the foundation for the future of bibliographic description that happens on the web and in the networked world. It is designed to integrate with and engage in the wider information community and still serve the very specific needs of libraries. (Bibliographic Framework Initiative, 2015)

Table 3.3
RDA-Required Areas of Description by MARC Tag

MARC Tag	RDA Core Elements	Example
010 020	Identifier for manifestation	13 ISBN 9718349289011
100	Creator	Houston, Cynthia, 1965-, author.
245	Title proper Statement of responsibility relating to title proper	Cataloging Dos and Don'ts / by Cynthia Houston.
250	Designation of edition	First edition.
260	Place of publication Publisher's name Date of publication Copyright date	Bowling Green, Ky. : WKU Press, Inc., 2014
300	Extent Specific Materials Designation Illustrative Content Dimensions Accompanying Material	xi, 255 pages ; 12 cm.
336 337 338	Media type Content type Carrier type	text unmediated volume
490	Series statement	
500	Summarization of the content	Common cataloging errors are discussed in a clear and concise manner

Paris Principles, International Standard for Bibliographic Description (ISBD), and Statement of International Cataloging Principles (ICP)

The Paris Principles, issued in 1961, were established to standardize how items are described in a catalog record. These principles specified spacing, capitalization, punctuation, and abbreviation rules for creating a catalog record. The ISBD is an outgrowth of the Paris Principles and specifies in detail how items are to be described. Because ISBD is an international standard, it allows catalog records from across the globe to be shared and displayed in a consistent and uniform style. According to Welsh and Bately (2012), ISBD is the key to universal bibliographic control for "even if we cannot read the language or script, we can identify the different areas of the catalogue record, because they are shown in the same order, with the same punctuation" (p. 20).

ISBD rules require the following eight elements for bibliographic description to be entered into the catalog record:

- Title and statement of responsibility
- Edition
- Material or type of publication

- Publication information
- Series information (if applicable)
- Notes (if applicable)
- Standard numbers and terms of availability (Welsh and Bately, 2012, p. 21)

In Figure 3.4, note where the eight elements are displayed in the catalog record.

The Statement of International Cataloging Principles (ICP) builds on policies established in the Paris Principles, but expands the vision and standards for universal bibliographic control to a 21st-century automated environment that contains an ever-increasing variety of information resources and formats. In nine simple declarations, these general principles express the need for library catalogs to serve the needs of users first and foremost:

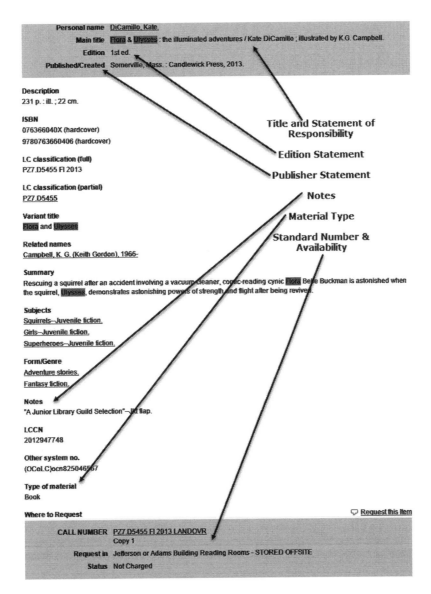

Figure 3.4. Catalog record and ISBD areas of description

1. Convenience of the user—bibliographic and authority descriptions should be created with the user in mind
2. Common usage—vocabulary for description should use commonly used terms
3. Representation—bibliographic and authority description should reflect how entity describes itself
4. Accuracy—entity should be portrayed accurately
5. Sufficiency and necessity—include data in descriptions sufficient to fulfill user tasks
6. Significance—data elements should be significant to the item described
7. Economy—use the lowest cost or simplest approach to achieving a goal
8. Consistency and standardization—access points should be standardized to ensure consistency
9. Integration—description for all types of materials should be based on a common set of rules (Statement of International Cataloging Principles, 2012)

Anglo American Cataloging Rules (AACR)

The AACR were also an outgrowth of the Paris Principles and became the set of rules used when creating catalog records for all types of items. These rules were in effect until the new RDA rules were adopted recently.

GUIDELINES FOR SCHOOL LIBRARIES

As professionals in the library science field, school librarians must recognize and follow accepted practices for cataloging and classification. However, because of the specialized nature of the school library organization and the users school libraries serve, there are some differences in some rules and procedures that must be followed relative to the catalog record, including purchasing records, copying catalog records from other sources, adding appropriate subject headings, and the use of the Dewey Classification System.

Typically, school librarians purchase catalog records from vendors who include them with their sales of library materials. In this case, school librarians typically add only local information such as the call number, bar code number, and local subject or curriculum information. If catalog records are not purchased, then school librarians can obtain records from other sources such as OhioLink, which is the statewide library consortium for Ohio, or the LC. Records from the other sources do not often contain subject headings appropriate for children. Therefore, school librarians may need to add subject headings from the *Sears List of Subject Headings*, which is designed specifically for schools and public libraries. Records from the LC and other sources also may use the LC Classification system rather than the DDC system that school libraries typically use for nonfiction items. For this reason, school librarians may need to add a DDC classification when creating local records or their library.

INTERNET RESOURCES

American Library Association. Association for Library Collections and Technical Services (ALCTS), RDA

http://www.ala.org/alcts/
http://www.ala.org/alcts/ianda/RDA

International Federation of Library Associations (IFLA) FRBR, ISBD, ICP

http://www.ifla.org/publications/functional-requirements-for-bibliographic-records
http://www.ifla.org/publications/international-standard-bibliographic-description
http://www.ifla.org/publications/statement-of-international-cataloguing-principles

Library of Congress MARC21, RDA, BIBFRAME

http://www.loc.gov/marc/bibliographic/
http://www.loc.gov/marc/umb/
http://www.loc.gov/aba/rda/
http://www.loc.gov/bibframe/

Online Computer Library Center (OCLC) WorldCat

https://www.oclc.org/worldcat.en.html

DISCUSSION QUESTIONS

1. Conduct a search for *Alice in Wonderland* using an online bookstore search feature and an Internet search engine; then use a library catalog such as the Library of Congress to conduct the same search. Compare and contrast your search experiences in terms of what information is displayed.
2. Discuss the strengths and weaknesses of international cooperation in creating cataloging standards. What do you think the bibliographic universe would look like without international standardization?
3. Review basic information from the websites associated with the national and international organizations discussed in this chapter. What kinds of cultural biases might we expect to see based on the participating members of these organizations? What are the implications for how much of the bibliographic universe can be described and included in library catalogs?

EXERCISES

1. Think of an example of an intellectual work or a creator of intellectual work and describe it in terms of FRBR Group 1 Entities and Attributes: work, expression, manifestation, and item.
2. Your library has received three copies of *Alice in Wonderland* by Lewis Carroll. One is a 1965 version of the book written by Lewis Carroll with illustrations by Andy Warhol, the second is a Disney movie, and the third is a Marvel Comics serialized graphic novel. Use the FRBR diagram from this chapter to create a diagram representing the different entities, attributes, and relationships of these three items.
3. Using the MARC record for the *Alice in Wonderland* book, label each of the fields that represent a specific RDA core element.
4. Create a chart with national and international organizations discussed in this chapter in one column and the rules they have developed and maintained in the second column. In the third column, explain the basic functions and activities of the organization in terms of the rules you have listed.

4

Subject Cataloging Principles and Procedures

INTRODUCTION

Take a moment to look around at all the living and nonliving things inhabiting the space you are in. If you had to describe the space to someone so that they would have a picture of your world, what terms would you use? Would you use a narrow term such as "office chair" or a broader term such as "furniture"? Would you use colloquial terms such as "snacks" or specific terms such as "granola bars"? These are the kinds of questions librarians who are engaged in subject cataloging ask themselves when they are trying to apply subject headings to describe items they want to include in the library catalog.

Librarians refer to the variety of items that can be included in a library catalog as "the bibliographic universe." The bibliographic universe is large and can contain many types of items, such as books, magazines, DVDs, websites, and streaming media. The number of items that can be included in the library catalog is expanding every second. As the bibliographic universe expands, the vocabulary we use to look for things in this universe also expands. For example, in the past, if you used an Internet search engine to look for information related to "tweets," you retrieved websites describing different kinds of bird songs. Now however, you will get these sites along with references to online messaging activities that take place using an online chat account, such as *Twitter*.

Because information now exists in print and electronic format, the library catalog has the potential to contain an infinite variety of items that are all a part of the bibliographic universe. This potentiality gives rise to the need for an information discovery system to manage the increasing amount of information added to the library's holdings. Librarians have used subject cataloging of some kind to manage their bibliographic universe for more than 100 years, beginning with Charles Cutter's *Rules for a Dictionary Catalog* in 1876. Subject cataloging is essentially a naming process for the purpose of organizing information for users of the library. Weihs and Intner (2009) describe subject cataloging as a process of determining what an item is about and assigning subject headings so that the item can be found in the catalog. A broader term used for this activity is "tag governance," which refers to the systematic use of "tags" for describing material primarily found online (Adamich, 2013). When librarians are engaged in subject cataloging or tag governance, they are attempting to group items together that share similar intellectual contents, so that users will be able to find most of the information they are looking for under one heading.

Table 4.1
Subject Cataloging Definition

Definition: Subject Cataloging
The process of providing subject access points to catalog records and subject headings to cataloging materials so that users can find like items easily.

SUBJECT CATALOGING IN THE SCHOOL LIBRARY

When you look at a catalog record, you will typically see subject terms at the bottom of the screen. Catalogers apply subject terms to describe the "aboutness" or the intellectual contents of an item. For example, in the Library of Congress catalog, the 1934 edition of the *Great Gatsby* by F. Scott Fitzgerald has the following subject headings, which comprise what the cataloger believes to be what the book is about: Traffic accidents, Married women, First loves, Rich people, Mistresses, Revenge, and Long Island (NY). In theory, these subject headings should provide a user who is searching for information on these topics to find a useful list of items available from the library. When librarians engage in subject cataloging, they are furthering Cutter's function for the library catalog, namely, to enable a user to find what the library has by the subject (Weihs & Intner, 2009). As part of their cataloging activities, librarians may need to add subject information, such as a more colloquial term, curriculum information, or additional authorized subject headings to make it easier for students to find items under headings they would be more likely to use.

SUBJECT HEADINGS AND THE SCHOOL LIBRARY CATALOG

In the age of ubiquitous Internet searching, why do librarians believe that subject cataloging is still an important activity? Typically, we enter a word or phrase that we think describes the information we are looking for into an Internet search engine and retrieve a list of results. Using this method, a number of results will be useful, and some will not be related to your search at all. This type of searching is called keyword or phrase searching and is used to find information using Internet search engines and library catalogs. Many library catalogs also have the option of searching by keyword or phrase as the default search option, but many libraries believe this is not always an effective way to search for information because this method does not use a controlled vocabulary, such as a list of subject headings to find information (Weihs & Intner, 2009).

Controlled Subject Heading Vocabulary

A controlled vocabulary is a precise list of terms or subject headings applied to each information item when it is being cataloged. The terms used in subject headings are agreed upon by a group of library professionals, updated regularly, and made available to libraries for their subject cataloging tasks. When a specific list of subject headings are used for subject cataloging, the list of terms is controlled so that related items can be found together. The controlled terms are the preferred terms used to describe that item of information and the term most commonly used (Broughton, 2004).

Along with keyword and phrase searching, the library catalog has as one of its search features the option to look for items by "subject heading." Use of subject headings in library catalogs provides a means for all items using that specific term to be retrieved together and therefore yields more precise results. An Internet search engine, such as *Google*, on the other hand, provides only keyword or phrase searching options and consequently yields an infinite list of less precise results. Furthermore, search engines often give priority to results from providers who have paid for their information to be on the top of the search results list, which diminishes their effectiveness as an information retrieval tool. Figure 4.1 shows where subject headings are listed in a library catalog record.

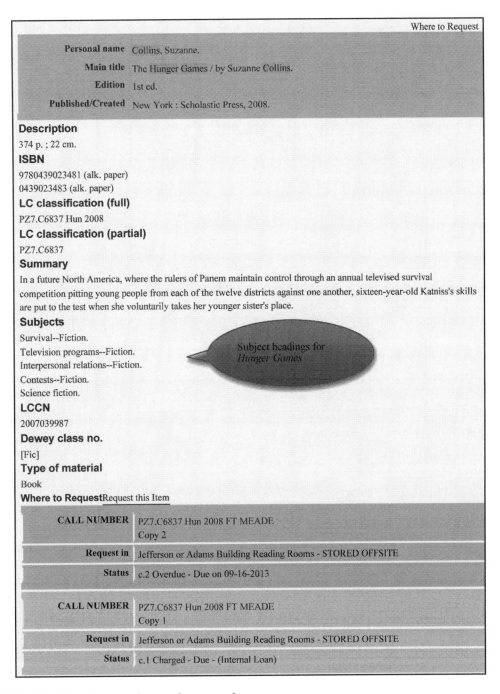

Figure 4.1. Subject headings in the catalog record

GENRES & TOPICS

apps Arithmetic -- Study and teaching Children's Literature Children-- Books and reading collaboration Core Content ELA core content Science Digital media digital storytelling Educational games Educational technology Elementary Elementary-education Encyclopedia games Geography High High School History Information technology Internet in education Knowledge management Language arts Library education Maps math Mathematics middle Middle/High School Middle Grades Middle School multimedia poetry presentations reading Reading--Phonetic method School libraries Science Skills Social sciences social studies Teaching-Aids and devices Technology Vocabulary Writing

Figure 4.2. Tag cloud example

Uncontrolled Subject Heading Vocabulary

An uncontrolled vocabulary is a list of terms used to describe items in a catalog that has no overarching controlling agency and involves no conscious decision making regarding what terms are added or deleted. Often, this vocabulary develops as a result of social tagging, in which users add their own descriptive terms to websites, pictures, catalog record, or other items found on the Internet (Baker, 2012). If you have applied a tag to a picture you posted on *Facebook* or a description of a book you listed on *GoodReads*, then you engaged in cataloging the Internet via the use of tagging. The use of tagging and tag clouds on the Internet are a means to identify commonly used keywords for particular items. The classification scheme resulting from these tagging activities are referred to as "folksonomies" because they are developed by a large population of users as opposed to a small group of people. Many Web 2.0 applications that allow tagging also compile the result of tagging activities and display them visually using a tag cloud. Although tagging does help with developing a socially created controlled vocabulary or folksonomy that may be more relevant to the needs of the user, the results are still less precise than when subject headings are used (Sullivan, 2013).

Examples of the use of tagging in the bibliographic universe are featured in many Internet resources including blogs and websites. Tagging activities result in tag clouds like the one shown here. The larger the word in a tag cloud, the more often the tag has been used to describe a particular item. Tag clouds have also been incorporated into library catalogs to help users find related information using terms other than subject headings.

SUBJECT CATALOGING RULES AND TOOLS

Subject Cataloging Rules: Cutter's Rules

When a librarian engages in the process of identifying and applying a subject heading from an official controlled vocabulary list of terms, the results are the product of a subject analysis. In these activities, librarians are referring to commonly used subject lists to locate terms describing the intellectual contents of the item they are cataloging. The way in which these subject lists are constructed is very important because this will affect how users are able to find information. In his

Rules for a Dictionary Catalog, Charles Cutter listed important desirable features of a subject heading list, including:

- A preference for the use of commonly used or natural language.
- Use of the heading was based on consensus or literary warrant.
- Preference for direct word order (serial killer as opposed to killer, serial). (Broughton, 2004)

Subject Cataloging Tools: Subject Heading Lists

There are several official sources for controlled vocabularies used in libraries including the *Library of Congress Subject Headings* (LCSH), the *National Library of Medicine Medical Subject Headings*, the *Library of Congress Children's Subject Headings*, the *Book Industry Study Group Subject Headings* (BISG), and the *Sears List of Subject Headings* (Sears). Most of the records for items in a school library will include subject terms from the *Library of Congress* or the *Sears* list, although more schools and public libraries are also using terms from the BISG list (Wagner, 2012). Regardless of what subject heading list is used, their common features include:

- The use of simple, compound, and complex headings that are determined by an organization or governing body.
- The alphabetical arrangement of the list.
- The use of cross references to point users to broader, narrower, or related terms. (Broughton, 2004)

A typical subject heading entry may comprise a single word such as animals, a compound phrase, such as natural history, or a complex heading such as stories in rhyme. The entry will often include cross-references to broader subject headings. For example, a broader term for a "traffic accident" is "accident." Entries will also include other terms the heading is used for, such as "car wrecks."

Most subject headings for items in a school library are included in electronic catalog records or are located in the CIP information. Electronic records will often contain both the *Sears* and LCSH headings, while the CIP information will most commonly list the LCSH because it is a publication of the Library of Congress. When school librarians must do their own subject cataloging, typically they use the *Sears* list as their standard reference. In comparing a subject heading search in *Sears* versus the Library of Congress, results from a *Sears* search will often yield fewer terms than a Library of Congress search. For example, a subject heading search for "aquarium" in the LCSH yields a long list of 31 subject headings, related to aquariums, while the same search using the *Sears* list provides two terms: "Aquariums" and "Marine aquariums." This is an example of how the *Sears* list of subject headings provides a simpler, more direct list of terms that may be more appropriate for subject cataloging tasks in school libraries. Because both lists are used in cataloging for school libraries, they will be described in this chapter. Specific steps for applying *Sears* subject headings for subject cataloging will also be addressed because this is an activity that school librarians will undoubtedly be engaged in at some point in their careers.

Library of Congress and *Sears Subject Headings*: Comparison and Contrast

The LCSH list was developed originally to manage the holdings of the U.S. Library of Congress, one of the world's largest libraries. Based on Cutter's principles outlined in the *Rules for a Dictionary Catalog*, the LCSH was instituted in 1898 and has been updated regularly to the present day. A list of subject headings is available online from the *Library of Congress Authorities* website. The list of subject headings currently contains more than 300,000 topical, personal, and geographic terms, and is as vast as the holdings of the Library of Congress (Fascinating Facts, n.d.). *The Library of Congress Children's Subject Headings* is a list of terms tailored to the needs of children and young adults for less technical terminology. The LCSH list is used for subject cataloging in research libraries with large holdings. Figure 4.3 is an example of an LCSH authority record for the subject heading used for "Cows." Notice that the authority record lists the preferred term, as well as narrower terms and references to other related subject headings.

Figure 4.3. Library of Congress authority headings

◄ Result List | Refine Search   ◄ 1 of 1 ►

Cattle

Geographic Note:	(May subdiv. geog.)
Dewey Classification:	599.64
	636.2
Use For:	Cows
Broader Terms:	Domestic animals
	Mammals
Narrower Terms:	Beef cattle
	Dairy cattle
AN:	150861

◄ Result List | Refine Search   ◄ 1 of 1 ►

Figure 4.4. *Sears* subject heading for cattle

The *Sears List of Subject Headings* (Sears) was developed by a single librarian, Minnie Earl Sears, in 1923 to manage the smaller holdings of school and public libraries. The *Sears* list is based on LCSH headings but with fewer compound headings and less technical terminology. The *Sears* list also incorporates the *Library of Congress Subject Headings for Children's Literature* to improve library patron access to children's material by subject (Adamich, 2013). Figure 4.4 is an example of a subject heading for "Cows" in the *Sears* list. Notice that in *Sears*, the preferred term for "Cows" is actually "Cattle," which is in contrast to the LCSH. However, like LCSH, *Sears* also has references to broader and narrower subject headings.

Although they are designed for different types of libraries, the LCSH and *Sears* lists have many similarities:

- Structure—both the Library of Congress and *Sears* subject headings have the same basic structure, using an alphabetical list of words used for subject cataloging.
- Organization—both lists resemble a thesaurus in that for most every word entry, there are references to narrower terms, broader terms, and preferred terms.
- Construction—in both cases, subject headings comprise single words, compound words, phrases, and complex headings, and make use of what is referred to as "structured headings" in which a subject heading is made more specific with the application of a topical, geographic, or free-floating subdivisions.
  - Topical subdivisions—in both *Sears* and LCSH, subject headings can be more narrowly defined with the use of subdivisions. For example, topics related to migrating geese may be narrowed by adding a subdivision "Migration patterns" to the main subject heading "Geese."
  - Geographic subdivisions—in both *Sears* and LCSH, subjects can be more narrowly defined by location; for example, topics related to California history can be narrowed by adding a geographic subdivision "California" to the main heading "History."
  - Free-floating subdivisions—both *Sears* and LCSH headings can be narrowed by adding non-geographic subdivisions that narrow down the topic by the form of the item (encyclopedia, dictionary, biography, etc.) by a particular group of people, such as women, or by chronology, such as 20th century; for example, topics related to women's history are narrowed by adding "Women" as a subdivision to the main heading "History."

A key difference between the LCSH headings and the *Sears* list is that *Sears* is designed for what Adamich (2013) refers to as "scalability" and "flexibility." While the vast list of LCSH terms are controlled by the Library of Congress, which imposes strict limitations on users' ability to add new terms, the *Sears* list provides a more streamlined list of terms with guidelines on creating new subject headings, patterns and examples for topical terms, and the use of chronological, geographic, and free-floating subdivisions. This feature allows librarians to add terms to their own catalogs to meet the needs of their community of users. Information on how librarians can create subject headings or narrow existing headings by the use of subdivisions is provided in the document "Front Matter" (2007) located in the front part of the printed volume of the *Sears List of Subject Headings* and as an electronic file in the online database. Because new subject headings can be created using guidelines from the *Sears* list, it has flexibility for adding less technical or more colloquial terms, making the discovery process easier for younger library users. The *Sears* list adds scalability in that as new topics appear, the basic list can be expanded either through the use of new headings or by adding subdivisions to existing terms.

Pets

Geographic Note:	(May subdiv. geog.)
Dewey Classification:	636.088
See Also:	types of common pets, e.g. Dogs; and types of animals not ordinarily kept as pets, e.g. Snakes as pets [to be added as needed]
Broader Terms:	Animals
Narrower Terms:	Snakes as pets
Related Terms:	Domestic animals
AN:	150897

Figure 4.5. *Sears* subject heading for pets

Another important difference between the LCSH and *Sears* is that *Sears* aligns its headings with the classification numbers in the *Abridged Dewey Decimal Classification*. Consequently, when a librarian uses *Sears* for subject cataloging, the Dewey Classification number or DDC is also listed with the subject heading. This feature simplifies the process of grouping items together by subject heading or Dewey Classification, as well as grouping them together in a physical location. Figure 4.5 shows the *Sears* subject heading entry for "Pets" and the associated Dewey Classification 636.088.

SUBJECT CATALOGING USING THE *SEARS LIST OF SUBJECT HEADINGS*

Structure and Organization of the Sears List

Using the *Sears* list for subject cataloging is a fairly straightforward task, made easier with practice. The print version of the *Sears List of Subject Headings* is organized much like a thesaurus. The terms are listed alphabetically, and for every term, there are references to narrower, broader, preferred, and non-preferred terms. For example, the *Sears* subject heading "Pets" has a "See also" or SA statement, directing users to search under common types of pets such as dogs. There are also narrower headings such as "Snakes as pets" and broader terms such as "Animals" listed. This heading also has a related term "Domestic animals" listed. All of these references help the cataloger with subject cataloging as they search through the headings and locate the most precise term that describes the item they are cataloging. The online version of the *Sears* list is available from the EBSCO Host Database Services. The online version makes searching for subject headings easier because the database search engine can be used to browse for headings. In addition, hyperlinks allow users to navigate between narrow and broad headings to find the most specific subject heading.

The *Sears* list organizes subject headings into the following types:

- Topical headings—headings that describe the subject of an item and can consist of one term such as "cats" or a short phrase such as "gun control."
- Form headings—headings that describe the format of an item, such as a "Dictionary" or "Encyclopedia," or a genre such as "Fiction" or "Essays."

- Geographic headings—headings that describe the geographical location or country.
- Name headings—headings that refer to people and companies.

The *Sears* list organizes subdivisions into different types that mirror the organization of the subject headings:

- Topical subdivisions—headings that express some aspect of the item.
- Geographic subdivisions—headings that express a location or country.
- Chronological subdivisions—headings that express a significant time period.
- Form subdivisions—headings that identify a specific format.

When creating catalog records, the following format is used for subject headings and subdivisions:

- The first letter of the subject heading is capitalized.
- Subject headings and subdivisions are separated by a double dash.
- The first letter of each subdivision is capitalized.
- The end of each subject heading entry is punctuated with a period.

For example, a subject heading for a textbook on school librarianship would look like this with a main heading and subdivision (table 4.2):

Table 4.2
Format for Subject Heading Entry

Library education—Study and teaching.

A number of subdivisions can be applied to an item for an increasingly more specific classification of an item. The order for listing subdivisions is as follows:

Subject Heading—Topical subdivision—Geographic subdivision—Chronological subdivision—Form subdivision.

Table 4.3 shows the subject heading for an atlas describing the locations of saber-toothed cats from the Pleistocene period in the United States:

Table 4.3
Subject Heading Entry for Topic with Multiple Subdivisions

Prehistoric animals—Wild cats—North America—Atlas.

RULES FOR APPLYING SUBJECT HEADINGS USING *SEARS*

Specific Entry and Unique Heading Rules

When engaged in subject cataloging, there is a definite procedure for searching for and applying subject headings. Two important principles are called the principle of "specific entry" and the principle of "unique heading." The idea behind subject cataloging is to describe the item using the most precise subject heading without applying a term that is too narrow or too broad, and to use that term consistently with new items added to the library catalog. Following the specific entry rule ensures that the most specific term that can be used to describe the item is the most preferred term. Following the unique heading principles ensures that only one term will be used for cataloging items dealing with the same subject matter. For example, in an item about dogs, the specific entry principle suggests that the more specific term "dogs" be used rather than the broader term "domestic animals." The unique heading rule asserts that in this case all items related to dogs should be placed under the subject heading "dogs." Using these two principles in applying subject heading will increase the chances that like items will be found together under the same term (Front Matter, 2007).

Scope Notes

Scope notes are included in subject headings when the meaning of the term requires clarification. Scope notes are commonly used in *Sears* when one term has different meanings in different contexts, such as "marketing," when distinctions need to be made between the subject heading as a topic and the subject heading as a form, as in "dictionary" and literary headings that refer to individual works (Front Matter, 2007).

SUBJECT CATALOGING STEP BY STEP USING THE *SEARS LIST OF SUBJECT HEADINGS*

STEP 1: Describe the intellectual contents.

The first step in applying subject headings is to determine the intellectual contents of the item by examining the title, table of contents, and the introduction, preface, or chapter headings to generate a draft list of subject headings. This activity will help focus the subject cataloging on specific subject headings that can be assigned to the item.

STEP 2: Select appropriate subject headings.

The next step is to locate appropriate terms from the *Sears* list, choosing the most specific term that can be used to describe the contents of the item. More subject headings can be applied, but the first term, because it is aligned with a Dewey Classification number, should most closely represent the intellectual contents of the item.

STEP 3: Review your selection.

The third step is to check the library catalog to see whether related items are assigned the same subject heading or whether another subject heading is used. This activity will help keep like items together in the catalog and on the library shelf.

STEP 4: Apply subdivisions.

Finally, if necessary, narrow the subject heading by applying subdivisions following instructions provided in *Sears* "Front Matter." An item can be made more specific by adding what are referred to as "subdivisions." For example, we can narrow the subject term "Pets" by applying a form subdivision for "Encyclopedia," yielding the subject heading "Pets—Encyclopedias."

STEP 5: Create a new subject heading.

If no appropriate subject heading exists in the *Sears* list, librarians are allowed to create new headings, but these must be saved in what is called a local authority file to ensure that future items on the topic will be assigned this new subject heading.

The *Sears* list is designed to be a basic tool for assigning subject headings as well as a guide for creating subdivisions and new subject headings. Although *Sears* is a subject heading list developed for school and public libraries, many of the headings use more advanced vocabulary than a young student might use to search for information. For example, the *Sears* list does not have a subject heading for "Swans" that would be appropriate for a book such as *The Ugly Duckling*. There is a subject heading for "Water birds" with a heading for "Terns" but no heading for "Swans." In this case, a librarian can add the subject heading to the library catalog and create a local authority record for "Swans." Tables 4.4 and 4.5 are sample local authority records.

Table 4.4
Subject Heading Entry with References

Subject Heading: Swans Narrow term: Black swan Broad term: Water birds
Subject Heading: Water Birds Narrow term: Black swan See also: Swans

Table 4.5
Authority Record for STEM

Subject Heading: STEM Broad term: Science—Study and teaching NOTE: Science, technology, engineering, and   mathematics
Subject Heading: Science—Study and Teaching See also: STEM

In addition to adding topical subject headings, there may be terms associated with the school curriculum that are not part of the *Sears* list but would be used by teachers and students to find information. For example, the *Sears* list does not have a subject heading for "STEM," the acronym for the curricular area of science, technology, engineering, and mathematics. *Sears* only has the broad subject heading "Science—Study and teaching," but this is not the term teachers would likely use to find materials related to STEM learning. To add "STEM" as a subject heading to the *Sears* list, a school librarian would add the heading to the catalog record and then create a local authority record for "STEM," with an explanatory scope note and a reference from "Science—Study and Teaching" to "STEM" as a narrow term.

SUBJECT CATALOGING FINAL THOUGHTS

Although subject cataloging using subject headings does seem to involve a lengthy and complicated process, it does make possible the finding and colocation functions of the library catalog as defined by Cutter. When searching for items using subject headings, all the items in the catalog related to that heading will be retrieved, and more than likely, they will be placed in the same location on the library shelf. Using subject terms to search for information is an important skill for students to learn because it will help them to develop their vocabulary related to a specific topic and to refine their information searching skills by understanding the relationship between subject headings, narrow and broad terms, and subdivisions. However, most subject heading lists are designed to serve a population that speaks English as their first language. With the growing number of native Spanish speakers in our schools, it is beneficial to add subject headings in Spanish. *Subject Headings for School and Public Libraries Bilingual Fourth Edition* (2012) was developed to provide a tool for adding Spanish subject headings to the library catalog.

INTERNET RESOURCES

Library of Congress Subject Headings

http://id.loc.gov/authorities/subjects.html

Book Industry Study Group Subject Headings

https://www.bisg.org/complete-bisac-subject-headings-2014-edition

Sears List of Subject Headings **Front Matter**

http://support.ebsco.com/downloads/resources/SearsFM.pdf

Library Thing Zeitgeist

http://www.librarything.com/zeitgeist

DISCUSSION QUESTIONS

1. In a nutshell, what are the differences between using a controlled vocabulary, such as *Sears*, and an uncontrolled vocabulary? What are the strengths and weaknesses of using subject headings to search for information as opposed to natural language searching?
2. How do you think teaching the use of subject headings as a search strategy would assist English language learners? How do you think adding subject headings in an English language learners' native language would help with the information search process?
3. Take a look at the tag cloud for the collections of items in Library Thing (https://www.librarything.com/tagcloud.php). Try to summarize the Library Thing collection based on the relative sizes of the tags. Does the tag cloud accurately describe the collection? Is this tag cloud useful for searching for items in Library Thing?
4. Take a look at the "Most popular tags" area in WorldCat (https://www.worldcat.org/). Does the tag cloud accurately describe the collection? Do you think this tag cloud is useful for searching for items in WorldCat?

EXERCISES

1. Subject cataloging—give subject cataloging a try by looking at the back of the title page (verso) of a recent nonfiction book and note the subject headings. Use the LC authorities to look up the subject headings. Then, use *Sears* subject headings to go through the same process. Note the DDC classification assigned to the subjects found in *Sears*. In an analysis, describe both subject headings tools, including similarities and differences.

2. Subject cataloging—pick the following one item description and identify appropriate *Sears* subject headings and Dewey Classification. In an analysis, cite the *Sears* subject headings, the DDC *Sears* assigns to this item, and subject headings that might be included in the local authority file for students.

   i. A picture encyclopedia for children, the text, and photos explore the history, development, and impact of automobiles from horseless carriages and Model T Fords to today's high-performance racing cars, featuring detailed cutaway photos showing how the moving parts of a car work.

   ii. A picture encyclopedia for children, the text, and photos explore the physical characteristics, behavior, and life cycle of various types of sharks.

   iii. A picture encyclopedia for children, the text, and photos explore the social life and customs, art, architecture, public works, and political and economic systems of ancient China.

   iv. The collections of stories and essays in this book present the Jack tales' popularity among traditional Appalachian storytellers and among storytelling revivalists.

   v. This book offers students the essential information they need to understand cultural anthropology, covering fundamental terms and issues included in all anthropology texts.

   vi. To show what effect Scottish participation has had on the nation of Canada, the work of 13 authors are included in this collection, tracing the history of the Scots in 14 different areas of Canadian life.

   vii. This textbook provides an overview of reference skills for school library media specialists, including teaching information literacy skills to specific categories of reference materials.

   viii. This textbook is an overview of library classification and cataloging, including subject classification, classification systems, and the AACR governing the cataloging of items for a library.

   ix. This book is an overview and criticism of the use of educational technology in schools across America. The author visited dozens of schools to present compelling tales about the misuse of teacher and student time and resources in the quest for the newest educational technology application.

5

Subject Classification Rules and Procedures

INTRODUCTION

Every day we are doing some kind of classification task. Whether we are shopping for items in a grocery or hardware store, sorting laundry, or organizing our computer files, all these activities involve identifying items we are looking for, locating them, and making decisions about their organization and relationships with one another. In libraries, classification is defined as a process of assigning a discipline or class to an item using a prescribed system of letters and numbers such as the Library of Congress or DDC systems (Table 5.1).

Classification provides an orderly and predictable arrangement for items on the library shelves. For example, a book about zoo animals would be classed in the discipline of natural sciences and shelved with other books about animals, while a book on the U.S. Civil War would be classed in the discipline of history with other books about the Civil War in the United States. In both cases, these items would be found on the library shelves among similarly classed items, making it easy for users to find items in their area of interest.

Classification schemes also allow users to search the automated catalog to find items related to each other regardless of their electronic or print formats. Ideally, library catalog users can browse for items by classification scheme and locate both print and electronic resources in their area of interest. Using a prescribed classification scheme in a library provides a predictable order for users to find information and furthers Cutter's goals for the library catalog—to enable a person to find a book when the subject is known, to show what the library has on a given subject, and to assist in the choice of a book as to its literary or topical character (Taylor, 2004).

Table 5.1
Definition of Library Classification

Library Classification is:
A process of assigning a discipline or class to an item using a prescribed system of letters and numbers such as the Library of Congress or DDC systems.

CLASSIFICATION SCHEMES IN LIBRARIES

There are several different classification schemes used in libraries today. In the United States, the Library of Congress Classification system is used in large academic libraries, while the Dewey Decimal Classification system is used in most public and school libraries. In Europe, the Universal Decimal Classification (UDC) system, based on the Dewey system, is used in school, public, and academic libraries.

The classification schemes used by libraries today have their roots in the outline of knowledge proposed by the 17th-century English scientific philosopher Francis Bacon. In the Baconian system, human knowledge comprises the three human faculties of memory, imagination, and reason, which are identified with three main intellectual disciplines: historical sciences, the poetical sciences, and philosophy (Taylor, 2000). The Baconian system of classification was used by the French in the 18th century and was employed by Thomas Jefferson when he developed the organization scheme for the Library of Congress collection, initially comprising Jefferson's donated books. In the 19th century, Melvil Dewey devised the DDC system based on this scheme (Taylor, 2000). The UDC system uses the main categories of the DDC, with adaptations for a multilingual society.

Although the LCC and DDC systems are based on the same underlying divisions of knowledge, they differ in how these divisions are ordered and the degree to which the divisions are split into narrower categories. The Library of Congress system uses letters and numbers in its classification system. For example, works related to library science are classed in the "Z" section, with a numeric notation for the subclasses, such as "Z48" for the subclass "Duplicating processes" (Library of Congress Classification Outline). The DDC uses only numbers with three decimal places. The DDC has 10 main classes from 000 to 900, summary tables for the hundreds division numbered from 000 to 990, and thousands section that are ordered from 000 to 999. So, for example, informational items about books are in 001, while information about geography and travel in the ancient world are classed in 913.

The UDC system uses a similar set of main classes as the Dewey system, except for the 400 foreign languages class, which is left vacant. This is because the UDC system is designed for collections containing works in multiple languages, while the Dewey system was designed for collections primarily in English. The summary tables for the hundreds and thousands division do class information differently from the DDC. For example, the UDC class 001 is for general works in science and technology, and the UDC class 913 is for regional geography.

To better understand the similarities and differences between these classification systems, Table 5.2 lists the main classes in the LCC, DDC, and UDC systems. Reviewing the table makes it easy to understand why the Library of Congress system, with its more expansive list of classifications, would be the preferred system for large academic libraries, while the smaller and simpler system used in the DDC would be preferred by smaller libraries serving the general public, and the UDC system is designed to accommodate libraries large and small that house collections in multiple languages.

It is also interesting to note that all of these classification systems divide the intellectual universe into an order reflecting a purely Western civilization orientation to knowledge and worldview. Furthermore, both the Dewey and Library of Congress

Table 5.2
Comparison of Library Classification Schemes

Library of Congress Classification	Dewey Decimal Classification	Universal Decimal Classification
A General works B Philosophy, psychology, religion C Auxiliary sciences of history D World history and history of Europe, Asia, Africa, Australia, New Zealand, etc.— E History of the Americas F History of the Americas G Geography, anthropology, recreation H Social sciences J Political science K Law L Education M Music and books on music N Fine arts P Language and literature Q Science R Medicine S Agriculture T Technology U Military science V Naval science Z Bibliography, library science, information resources (general)	000 Computer science, information, and general works 100 Philosophy and psychology 200 Religion 300 Social sciences 400 Language 500 Science 600 Technology 700 Arts and recreation 800 Literature 900 History, geography, and biography	000 Generalities 100 Philosophy, psychology 200 Religion, theology 300 Social sciences 400 Vacant 500 Natural sciences 600 Technology 700 The arts 800 Language, linguistics, literature 900 Geography, biography, history

systems reflect an Anglo American representation of knowledge in that they categorize any work in a language other than English in the 400s class regardless of topic. This bias has become an issue for library professionals as resources from other language and culture groups are being integrated into online library catalogs such as WorldCat that serve a worldwide population (Taylor, 2000).

DDC IN DETAIL

The DDC system was first developed by Melvil Dewey in 1876 for Amherst College in Massachusetts. Currently, the DDC is owned by the OCLC and used by most school and public libraries in the United States (Bowman, 2005). The DDC is a hierarchical scheme comprising a set of main classes from 000 to 900, representing academic disciplines; each main class has 10 subordinate divisions representing different fields of study within a discipline. For example, the DDC class for general science is 500, mathematics is 510, astronomy is 520, and so on. Within each division are subordinate sections narrowing the area further. For example, in the 530 division, the 531 class is for classical mechanics and the 532 class is for fluid mechanics. A decimal point follows the first three digits and provides a means for more specific classification within a section. The Dewey Summaries provide an overview of the classification system, listing the 10 main classes, the hundreds divisions, and the thousands sections (Dewey, 2012).

There are two versions of the DDC, the multivolume full version used in libraries with large collections and the single volume *Abridged* version used in school and small public libraries. In both versions, the organization system uses the summaries that include classifications for all subjects from 000 to 999, schedules for each classification number, and tables that provide additional numbers that can help place like items together within a particular classification.

To determine the precise Dewey Classification for an item, the discipline or field of study of the work must be determined using the Dewey Summaries, Schedules, and Tables. This is a time-consuming and complicated process typically not done by school librarians. In the circumstances where classification must be done in the school library, the *Abridged Dewey Decimal Classification*, along with the *Sears List of Subject Headings*, is an excellent resource (Bristow & Farrar, 2014).

CLASSIFICATION STEP BY STEP

There is a specific process for classifying a work using the DDC, which starts with determining the subject of a work, the discipline of a work, and any other facet of the work important in classification. This section summarizes the classification process and can assist beginning catalogers with understanding the process, but does not delve into the detail required to understand or apply the *Abridged Dewey Decimal Classification*.

STEP 1: Determine the subject—determine the subject of the work by examining the table of contents, preface, introduction, and any other useful information about the item.

STEP 2: Identify subject heading—consult the *Sears List of Subject Headings* to identify the main heading for the item and suggested DDC.

STEP 3: Consult DDC—consult the DDC Summaries to verify the classification suggested by the *Sears* list.

- Consult the DDC Schedules to narrow the classification further.
- If appropriate, add numbers from the DDC tables to reflect information about the geography or form of an item. Specific instructions on using the tables for number building are in the introductory chapter of the *Abridged* version of the DDC. There are four tables used to determine subdivisions:

  o Table 1—standard subdivisions, representing the physical form of an item, such as a dictionary or encyclopedia, or approach, such as history or research.

o Table 2—geographic areas and persons, generally used along with the 09 notation from Table 1 to designate historical, geographical, or biographical treatment of the item.
o Table 3—individual literatures and specific literary forms, used in the 800s class to designate specific forms of literature such as poetry.
o Table 4—individual languages, used within the 400s class to designate specific languages.

Table 5.3 describes the step-by-step process of classifying a work on the food customs of 20th-century Algeria.

Table 5.3
Using the *Sears* List and Abridged DDC for Classification

Steps	Actions	Result
STEP 1: Identify intellectual contents: food customs, Algeria, 20th century	Consult the Table of Contents, Preface, or any useful summary information	Topic: food customs of 20th-century Algeria
STEP 2: Consult the *Sears List of Subject Headings* for main heading and suggested DDC	A search in the *Sears* list for a main subject heading yields: "Food customs" with a DDC of 394.1	394.1 Food customs
STEP 3: Consult the DDC summaries to verify classification suggested by Sears.	Consulting the Summaries yields: 300 Social Sciences; 390 Customs, etiquette, and folklore; 394 General customs	394 General customs
STEP 3: Consult the DDC schedules for narrower classification and verify base number	Consulting the Schedule for 394 yields 394.1 Eating, drinking, using drugs	394.1 Eating and drinking
STEP 3: Consult Table 1 to add notation for historical treatment	Consulting Table 1 yields the notation of .09 for historical, geographic, persons treatment	394.109 Geographic treatment
STEP 3: Consult Table 2 to add notation for geography	Consulting Table 2 yields the notation of 65 for Algeria	394.10965 Algeria

CREATING CALL NUMBERS

The task of classification ensures that related items in the library catalog can be found together. In an automated cataloging environment, this means that physical and virtual items can be added to the catalog. Because they do not need to be shelved in the library's collection, virtual items, such as eBooks and webpages, typically do not have location information added to their record. However, to find an item on the library shelf, some kind of notation scheme is needed for the user to locate items found in the catalog within the physical holdings of a library. It is for this reason that items in the library have a call number, so that every item in the collection will have a unique location on the shelf.

In large academic libraries, call numbers comprise the LCC, the date of the work, and other distinguishing numbers representing the title and author of the work. In school and public libraries, fiction and nonfiction items are typically shelved in separate areas, and different classification schemes are used. In school libraries, each individual item of nonfiction is assigned a call number using the DDC, publication date, and a notation system signifying the title and author of the work. Works of fiction are commonly organized by author, while autobiographies, individual biographies, and collected biographies are done in different ways—by classifying them in the 920s area of the DDC, by placing them in the subject area in which the biographee (the person featured in the biography) is associated, or by creating a separate biography section and arranging the titles by the last name of the biographee.

Because the clientele of school and public libraries are children and the general public, call numbers must be kept as simple as possible. Individual libraries often will develop their own systems for assigning call numbers based on the DDC, publication date, and author. For this reason, call numbers for the same item may differ from library to library. When items are given DDC numbers by catalogers, they sometimes will be segmented to allow libraries the option of using a longer or shorter number (Table 5.4). The segmentation marks are either a prime symbol ' or a forward slash / and show where the number can be shortened or lengthened. For example, Table 5.4 shows how segmentation marks in a DDC of 341.75'30 instruct the cataloger to use the shorter number 341.75 rather than the longer number 341.7530.

Table 5.4

Segmentation Example

Segmented Instructions for DDC classification: 341.75'30
Full classification number: 341.7530
Segmented classification number: 341.75

Depending on the size of the collection and age of the clientele, school libraries typically use the call numbering system given in Table 5.5 for fiction and nonfiction items.

In many cases, library collections house different works on a subject by the same author, or works on the same subject by authors with the same last name. For these reasons, call numbers have additional notation systems. Nonfiction call numbers sometimes use a Cutter number after the Dewey classification and a work mark after the Cutter number. The Cutter number is a code that comprises the letters in an author's name to assist with ordering items by the author. The work mark is the first letter of the book's title and assists with ordering items by the same author alphabetically according to title. The advantages of using Cutter numbers, work marks, and publication dates are that books by the same author will be placed together on the shelf in a logical order.

Table 5.5
Call Numbering Systems Typical of School Libraries

	Fiction/Easy Fiction	Nonfiction /Biography/ Easy Nonfiction/ Reference	Languages Other Than English	Other Materials
Options	*Fiction* F with first one to three letters of author's surname FIC with first three letters of author's surname First three letters of author's surname *Easy Fiction* E with first one to three letters of author's surname	*Nonfiction* Classification number with first one to three letters of author's surname *Biography* B with first three letters or all of biographee's surname 92 with first three letters of biographee's surname 920 with first letter of author's surname (collected biography) 921 with first three letters or all of biographee's surname (individual biography) *Easy Nonfiction* E above classification number for all Easy Nonfiction *Reference* R or Ref above assigned classification number R or REF above assigned classification number with first one to three letters of author's surname	Classification number assigned by subject Language code with first one to three letters of author's surname Language code with classification number assigned by subject	Audiovisual Graphic Novels Professional Development
Examples	*The Mouse in the House* by Jerri Smith F Smi F Smith E Smi E Smaith J Smi	*Pilgrims in New England* by John Smith 974.4 Smith *The Life of John Smith* by Pat Jones 92 Smi 921 Smith *The Smiths of New England* by Pat Jones 920 Jones	*Los Tarahumaras* by Maria Gomez 972.004 Gomez Sp Gom Sp Gomez Sp 972.1 Gomez	AV PD

PROCEDURES FOR CREATING CALL NUMBERS IN SCHOOL LIBRARIES

Typically, book suppliers for school libraries will offer different options for call numbers when they create spine labels and electronic records for the books ordered by the school. It is important for school librarians to know and understand the different components of a call number in order to make professional decisions about changes or corrections that must be made to comply with professional standards. For example, in the case where a new collection is developed for a large K-12 library, the librarian has the responsibility to make a decision about the call numbering system to be used. For picture books, chapter books, and biographies, this decision is relatively easy and could use the system described in this chapter. For nonfiction books, librarians should refer to the *Abridged Dewey Decimal Classification* and the *Sears List of Subject Headings* for the Dewey classification, to the publication date and title of the item for the appropriate date and work mark and, if required, to the print or online table of Cutter numbers for the Cutter Number. The free Cutter—Sanborn Tables Program is available from OCLC at their website. Table 5.6 provides examples of call numbers for fiction, nonfiction, biographies and audiovisual materials.

ALTERNATIVE CLASSIFICATION

The DDC system, as a means to organize a school or public library, has been widely criticized by both librarians and their users because it is difficult for young people to understand the three-digit system, reinforces an English language and Western bias toward knowledge, does not accommodate items that deal with multiple subjects, and sometimes does not keep items that are interdisciplinary together (Jameson, 2013). Librarians using the DDC for cataloging also experience frustrations with the system because some main classes are more thoroughly divided into subdivisions than others. For example, the divisions for the 100s class, dealing with philosophy, are quite broad, while divisions in the 600s class are continuously subdivided because of the growth of information in the technology subject area (Bowman, 2005). Furthermore, because subdivisions express different aspects of a topic—such as animals in religion or animals as pets—books on the same subject may end up in different areas of the library, making them difficult to find.

Because many school librarians and library users find the DDC difficult to navigate, alternative classification schemes have been proposed and implemented throughout the United States. Alternative classification systems implemented in school or public libraries use either the "Bookstore model," which uses genres and subject headings used by the Book Industry Study Group (BISG), or a child-centered classification scheme called "Metis" named after a character in Greek mythology related to wisdom and deep thought (Kaplan, Giffard, Still-Schiff, & Dolloff, 2013).

School librarians' difficulties with Dewey prompted editors of the American Association of School Librarians to dedicate a special issue of *Knowledge Quest* to this topic in 2013. Librarians weighed in on these matters with a debate ranging from retaining the DDC system because it was widely used and understood, to using the DDC only for nonfiction and genre classification for fiction, to interfiling fiction and nonfiction and using the BISG or Metis classification systems for the whole library.

Bookstore Model

The classification system based on genres is generally called the Bookstore model because it uses subject headings developed by BISG and arranges the library similar to the way bookstores arrange their stock, with fiction divided into mystery, romance, science fiction, and so on, and nonfiction arranged by subjects such as science, technology, history, and hobbies. In many of these systems, the call numbers use words

Table 5.6
Building Call Numbers for Library Items

Fiction	Nonfiction/Reference	Biography	Audiovisual
A Day on the Dairy Farm by John Smith, 2015	*Raising Cattle* by John Brown, 2015	*A Life on the Dairy Farm: John Smith*, 2015 by John Brown	*A Day on the Dairy Farm: A Documentary,* Paramount Pictures, 2015 *A Day on the Dairy Farm: The Movie,* Paramount Pictures, 2015
1. Select an abbreviation for Fiction such as F, Fic, or E for Easy Fiction, etc. This is typically already decided by the library: Fic Fic Smith	1. Create the DDC classification as described in this chapter 636.2	1. Identify where the biography is to be shelved, with Animal Husbandry 636.2, with biographies of scientists, 925, or in a separate section with the abbreviation of B for biography: B 636.2 925 B	1. Select an abbreviation for AV materials such as AV, DVD, and CD. This is typically already decided by the library: DVD
2. Identify the publication date: Fic Smith 2015	1. (Optional) Create a Cutter number using a chart or Cutter program. 2. 636.2 B8121	2. Add the name of the biographee: Smith	2. Select additional notation, such as classification for documentary films, or titles for dramas, cartoons, etc. DVD 636.2 DVD *Day*
	3. Create a work mark for the title using the first letter of the title that is not a, an, or the 636.2 B8121r	3. Add the publication date: 2105	3. Add the production date: 2105 DVD 636.2 2015 DVD *Day* 2015
	4. Add publication date 636.2 B8121r 2015		
	Reference Items Only 5. Add a notation for Reference, either R or REF or some combination R 636.2 B8121r 2015		
	When there is no author for an item, such as a collected work of nonfiction essays, the Cutter number is derived from the title of the work, and there is no work mark.	In school libraries, biographies are often shelved in a separate section. In a larger public library, biographies are shelved either with the topic of the person being written about or in a special DDC 920s section devoted to biography.	There is a wide variety of call numbering systems for audiovisual and other electronic materials used by libraries. This example is just for illustrating how a system is typically constructed.

rather than numbers that can be easily understood by young patrons. An example of how the Bookstore model was implemented can be found in in the Anythink libraries serving Denver, Colorado. Their first step was to identify user-friendly categories for their items using the BISG subject headings. Then, each item was revised in the automated catalog with the BISG term entered into the local call number field, relabeled and re-shelved in the library (Buchter, 2013).

Child-Centered Model—Metis

With the goal of creating a child-centered, easy-to-browse, and flexible means for students to navigate their 20,000-volume library, school librarians at the Ethical Culture Fieldston School in New York City developed the Metis classification model. In this scheme, the users of the library were polled about what categories would best fit the information needs of the students and came up with a list of whole-word categories for fiction, such as "Scary," "Adventure," and "Fantasy," as well as nonfiction categories such as "Machines," "Community," and "Making Stuff" (Kaplan et al., 2013). The librarians report that the reclassification of their library has made their students more independent users of information, has decreased the amount of time they spent on information location instruction, and has increased their time spent on information literacy instruction.

CLASSIFICATION FINAL THOUGHTS

School librarians are always looking for ways to organize their libraries to meet the needs of their users. For this reason, a number of classification schemes have been developed over the years including the Dewey classification, Genre or Bookstore classification, and the very intriguing Metis model. While these schemes vary in the way books are labeled and arranged on the shelves, students are still able to use the library catalog to browse and locate items in their interest areas, and the library catalog remains an essential tool for information literacy instruction.

INTERNET RESOURCES

Cutter Number program—Program from OCLC that generates Cutter numbers

http://www.oclc.org/support/services/dewey/program.en.html

WebDewey—Subscription-based online DDC classification program from OCLC

http://www.oclc.org/en-US/dewey/features.html

Digital Libraries to School Libraries—Tools for school librarians to integrate digital content into their catalogs

http://dl2sl.org/

DDC Updates—Updates on the DDC and related classification tools

http://ddc.typepad.com/

DISCUSSION QUESTIONS

1. Suppose you were given the opportunity to create a library for your school. What classification system would you choose for your library? Would you use the DDC or an alternative system? Explain your reasoning from the standpoint of how these systems serve those who are using your library.
2. You have been asked your opinion on interfiling books, periodicals, and audiovisual materials together on the library shelves. Explain your opinion on this matter using the rationale of how users look for information. Describe the classification scheme you would use for organizing your library, including the notation system you would use to distinguish between print and electronic materials.

EXERCISES

1. Create a classification number—select one of the listed titles to classify. Decide whether the item is fiction, nonfiction, or biography, then use the steps discussed in the chapter to classify the item using the *Sears List of Subject Headings* and the *Abridged Dewey Decimal Classification*.

   - *My life in libraries* by Melvil Dewey, 1935
   - *Muppy learns to count* by Buffy Smith, 2015
   - *How to train carrier pigeons* by Birdy Jones, 2000
   - *Dilbert take a bath* by Wally Brown, 2006
   - *Library classification for science fiction* by Channing Lois, 2000
   - *Accounting made easy* by Mark Counts, 2009
   - *The history of the United States Post Office* by Clarence Stamps, 2000
   - *Cows I have known: an autobiography* by Bovinius Abrams, 2014
   - *When the sun sets over New York: a novel* by Bloomberg Rockefeller, 2015
   - *Young adult fiction in the United States* by Blume Comier, 1999

6

Descriptive Cataloging: Rules, Procedures, and Practices

INTRODUCTION

Every school ILS has a cataloging module or component for editing existing items and adding new items to the library catalog. Typical cataloging activities school librarians engage in include importing catalog records purchased from book vendors into their ILS and editing them to include local information such as subject headings and local call numbers. Activities may also include creating new records by copying records from identical items found in other libraries or creating original records from start to finish. All of these functions can be completed using the cataloging module in the ILS (Intner & Weihs, 2015).

GENERAL RULES FOR DESCRIPTIVE CATALOGING

As discussed in previous chapters, cataloging practices in libraries are guided by professional standards established and agreed upon by professional library organizations. These standards and practices ensure that catalog records will be created with consistency so they may be shared between libraries. Also discussed briefly was the international standard for formatting catalog records as computer data files referred to as "MARC." All libraries sharing records as part of a cataloging consortia use the MARC format for their electronic records. All school library automated systems use the MARC format as well (Fountain, 2011).

Descriptive cataloging is the activity librarians engage in when they are creating a verbal description of an item to develop a catalog record. Until 2013, the AACR published by the Joint Steering Committee for Revision of AACR, Canadian Library Association, Chartered Institute of Library and Information Professionals, and the ALA governed professional standards for descriptive cataloging. Recently, standards have been revised and cataloging practice is guided by two standards documents known as the Functional Requirements for Bibliographic Description (FRBR) and Resource Description and Access (RDA). These documents, published by IFLA and the ALA, reflect the global nature of library catalogs, as well as changes in the library catalog technology. All of these standards guide librarians in how catalog information such as the title, author, format, and dimensions of an item are transcribed and entered into a catalog record (Intner & Weihs, 2015; Kelsey, 2014).

RDA rules outline specific practices and procedures for cataloging. Because school librarians are primarily engaged in copy cataloging, in which existing catalog records are used to create local records, a general understanding of the RDA rules is necessary for carrying out cataloging activities. The 2013 Revised edition of *RDA: Resource Description and Access* outlines the rules to follow when using RDA standards for cataloging tasks:

- Preferred source of information—Chapter 2—RDA rules explain that information used for descriptive cataloging should be transcribed or recorded from specific locations, including the title page for printed items, the cover or container for audio items, the title screen for moving images, and the website home page for Internet items.
- Core RDA elements—Chapter 0—it is important to include information in all the RDA core element fields in the record so that the item is complete, follows a uniform format, and can be shared with other libraries. Core elements include the following: title; statement of responsibility; series and serials statements; production, publication, manufacture, distribution, and copyright information; standard numbers; carrier type; and the extent of the item.

In addition to these core elements, librarians include additional information in their records such as call number, notes, and subject headings to aid the finding function of the library catalog.

- Representation principle—Chapter 1—referred to as the "take what you see" approach, this principle reminds catalogers to keep in mind that the catalog record should "reflect the resource's representation of itself." In other words, the record should be a mirror of the item and reflect what the cataloger sees on the preferred source of information rather than a rearrangement of this information.
- Transcription *vs.* recording—Chapter 1—the rules emphasize that catalogers should understand RDA guidelines related to transcribing *vs.* recording and the cases in which the guidelines need to be applied. For example, RDA differentiates *transcribing* information as it is presented in the title and edition statements, from information about the carrier type of the item, which is *recorded* using RDA prescribed format.
- Abbreviations—Appendix B—RDA rules state that in general, catalogers should not use abbreviations. For example, edition information or publisher information is not abbreviated unless it is displayed in that format on the item. Also abbreviations are no longer used when recording the extent of the item, except for dimensions (in. and cm) and duration (hrs. and min.).

MORE ON THE CORE: RDA CORE ELEMENTS

RDA also provides the type and format for entering information in the core element areas of the catalog record. In this way, there is consistency in the way the intellectual content of the items, their format, mode of communication, and their relationships with other works are described and displayed in the catalog. Each of these will now be discussed in detail. A summary sheet of key information related to RDA rules, MARC records, and formatted examples are included in the Appendix of this book.

1. Title—Chapter 2—also called the main title or title proper, this element is where the title information is entered. RDA rules require that titles be *transcribed* as they appear on the preferred source of information. The title page is the preferred source of information for print items and Internet resources. The title screen is the preferred source of information for films and videos, while the cover or case is the preferred source of information for audio materials. Following the principle of representation, capitalization and punctuation should appear in the way it is listed on the item. RDA does allow libraries to vary this rule to meet local standards because some libraries have their own capitalization and punctuation rules or use the rules listed in the *Chicago Manual of Style* (Intner & Weihs, 2015; Jacox et al., 2014). In this book, we will follow the representation principle and transcribe title information as depicted on the preferred source of information.

2. Statement of responsibility—Chapter 2—this element is one of the places where author or creator information is entered into the catalog record. Information for this element is transcribed from the preferred source of information. RDA rules allow for all the authors or creators listed on the preferred source of information to be included, but this is not a strict requirement. In a MARC catalog record, the title and statement of responsibility are listed together in the 245 field. The format follows the ISBD rules for punctuation located in RDA Appendix D:

    245   Title: subtitle / First statement of responsibility; Second statement of responsibility.

As an example, the title and statement of responsibility for *Alice in Wonderland* would be entered in the following manner:

    245   Alice's Adventures in Wonderland / Lewis Carroll; illustrated by John Tenniel.

In a MARC record, information about the creator of a work is also entered into the 100 field and is typically referred to as the main entry. When the creator is an individual author, the entry is made last name first, along with the creator's birth and death dates, and relationship designator. For the purpose of consistency, catalogers use the Library of Congress Name Authorities to locate the authorized name heading, birth dates, and death dates. RDA rules specify the specific relationship designators to be used to describe the creator, such as author, illustrator, or narrator. If there is more than one creator, additional entries may also be added to the record in the 700 field. ISBD punctuation rules apply to the main and added entries. The RDA Summary Sheet in the Appendix of this book provides assistance with this MARC field (Intner & Weihs, 2015; Jacox et al., 2014).

A main entry and additional entry typically follow this pattern:

    100   Last name, First name, birth date–death date, relationship designator.

A sample entry for the author and illustrator of an *Alice in Wonderland* book is listed in the following manner:

    100   Carroll, Lewis, 1832–1898, author.
    700   Tenniel, John, 1820–1914, illustrator.

If the creators are a corporate body such as a musical group, the information is recorded in the 110 and 700 fields of the MARC record. The 110 field is used for the corporate name of the group, while the 700 fields list the individual group members. The format for entering information about a corporate body typically follows this pattern:

    110   Group name (type of group)
    700   Last name, First name, birth date–death date, relationship designator.

A sample entry for a musical group is listed in the following manner:

    110   Beatles (musical group)
    700   Harrison, George, 1943–2001, performer.
    700   Lennon, John, 1940–1980, performer.
    700   McCartney, Paul, performer.
    700   Starr, Ringo, performer.

3. Edition Statement—Chapter 2—the edition statement lists information about the item's number of printings or special edition information and appears in the 250 field of the MARC record. Edition information is transcribed from the preferred source of information but is not always present (Intner & Weihs, 2015; Jacox et al., 2014). Examples of how edition information is entered in a catalog record include the following:

    250   Third edition.
    250   Special Anniversary Edition.
    250   5th edition.

4. Production, publication, distribution, manufacture information, and publication or copyright dates—Chapter 2—these elements provide information about the publishers, manufacturers, or distributors of the item and also the date of publication, manufacture, or copyright. In MARC records, this element appears in the 264 field and includes information about the publisher, manufacturer, or distributor, their location, and date of publication or copyright. Names and places are to be transcribed from the preferred source of information, and entries must include the city and larger jurisdiction such as state, province, or country. When publication dates are not listed, but a copyright date is listed, enter the copyright date in brackets and list the copyright date in a separate 264 field with the copyright symbol ©. This RDA core element is noted in a catalog record in the following format:

    264   City, State: Publisher name, publication date.

Here are two examples of an entry for this element:

    264   Santa Barbara, Calif. : Libraries Unlimited, [2015]
    264   @2015
    264   New York: Penguin Press, 2011.

5. Series statement—Chapter 2—a series statement describes the item as part of a series and, although required, is not always in a catalog record because not all items are part of a series. In cases when an item is part of a series, the information as it is listed on the item is recorded in the 490 MARC field. Along with the series statement, the 830 MARC field for the Uniform Series Title must be used with the 490 field to transcribe the series statement from the preferred source of information; the series number is also included when present. Enter the formal title of the series in the 830 field. The Library of Congress Authorities will assist with locating the uniform title of many series. The format for entering this information uses ISBD rules and typically follows this pattern:

490   Series name; series number
830   Series Uniform Title.

Examples of series statements include the following:

490   Green Thumb; volume 2
830   Green Thumb Series.

6. Identifier for the manifestation—Chapter 2—standard numbers such as a book's ISBN number, a serial's ISSN number, an audiovisual item's publisher number, or any other internationally recognized standard number are listed in this element. Using an identifying number is an important way to denote that a particular item is distinct from other versions of the same item. RDA rules state that this information can be taken from any place on the item. Identifier information is listed in the 010 (LCCN number), 020 (ISBN number), 022 (ISSN number), 024 (Other number, such as the Universal Product Code 12 digit bar code), and 028 (Publisher number) MARC fields depending on the format and content of the item. Transcribe the number as it appears on the item except in the case of ISBN numbers. When recording the ISBN number in the catalog record, all dashes separating the numbers are removed. Here are a few examples of identifier statements:

010   8401–8492
020   9789070002343
022   0046–225X
024   123456 789999
028   VU098

7. Extent—Chapter 3—an item's extent is basically a description of the item as a cataloger is viewing it in either physical or electronic form. This element provides information about the nature of the item. No abbreviations are used when entering information except for the duration (hrs. or min.) or length (in. or cm) of the item. Information about the extent of an item is included in the 300 MARC field of a catalog record. RDA rules require that ISBD punctuation be used when entering information about the extent of an item. Typically, the format of an item follows this pattern:

300   extent: illustrative content, illustrative content; dimensions + accompanying material.

Here are a few examples of MARC entries for the extent of different types of items:

300   150 pages : color illustrations; 24 cm
300   1 videodisc (45 min.): digital, stereo; 12 cm + insert.
300   1 online resource: color illustrations, sound.

8. Mode of Issuance, Content, Media, Carrier Type—Chapter 3—these core elements describe the manner in which information is delivered, how information is displayed, the format of the contents, and any media required to view the item. RDA prescribes specific terminology for recording these core elements in the catalog record. The Mode of Issuance refers to the manner in which the item is delivered, including a single unit such as a book, video program, or audio CD; a multipart monograph, such as a print encyclopedia; a serial, such as a magazine or journal; and an integrating resource, such as a website. When determining the Mode of Issuance, it is a good idea to think about whether or not the item is a complete physical or logical unit (single unit), whether information is broken into separate units (multipart monograph), whether an item is issued with stated frequency of publication (serial), or whether information is subject to regular updating by replacing information (integrating resource). The Mode of Issuance is noted in the LDR/07 MARC field of a MARC catalog record and is automatically entered into the record when the cataloger selects a specific type of item to catalog using the cataloging module of the ILS. The MARC notations for different modes of issuance are **m** (monograph) for single units such as books and multipart monographs, **s** (serial) for serials such as magazines, and **i** (integrating resource) for items that are regularly updated such as websites.

The Content Type of an item refers to the format of information contained in the item such as text, still images, audio, or video. Typically, the contents of an item can be determined by viewing the item itself. RDA rules have prescribed terminology to use for this element. Table 6.1 shows the Mode of Issuance and Content, Media, and Carrier Types typically associated with certain items. Content Type is noted in the 336 field of the MARC record and may include more than one entry depending on the nature of the item. A typical entry for the content type of a print item with illustrations follows this pattern:

336   text
336   still image

The Media Type of an item refers to the mediating equipment necessary to access information from the item. In the case of print materials, no equipment is required, and therefore the Media Type is "unmediated" in the 337 MARC field. RDA prescribes specific terminology for listing this information. A sample Media Type entry for a computer video game is listed as follows:

337   computer

Carrier Types denote the format of the storage medium associated with the item and is noted in the 338 field of the MARC record using prescribed RDA terminology. For example, the Carrier Type for an audio program on a CD is listed as an "audio disc." Here is an example of how the Carrier Type for a website is recorded in the MARC record:

> 338   online resource

Table 6.1 will assist beginning catalogers with identifying the Mode of Issuance, Content, Media, and Carrier Types for typical library materials.

Table 6.1
Common Library Resources, Mode of Issuance, Content, Media, and Carrier Types

Resource	Mode of Issuance	Content Type	Media Type	Carrier Type
print book	single unit in MARC **m**	text still image	unmediated	volume
online electronic Book	single unit in MARC m	text still image	computer	online resource
audio book on CD	single unit in MARC m	spoken word	audio	audio disc
music downloaded file	single unit in MARC m	performed music	computer	online resource
Print multivolume encyclopedia, dictionary, etc.	multipart monograph in MARC m	text still image	unmediated	Volume
Electronic encyclopedia, dictionary, etc. on CD-ROM	single unit in MARC m	text still image audio video	computer	computer disc
Print periodical	Serial in MARC s Individual Issues m	text still image	unmediated	Volume
Electronic Periodical online	Serial in MARC s Individual Issues m	text still image audio video	computer	online resource
Audiovisual production in audio or videodisk format	single unit in MARC m	two-dimensional moving image performed music	audio video	audio disc videodisc
Website, blog, or other Internet resource that is updated regularly	integrating resource in MARC i	text still image spoken word two-dimensional moving image performed music	computer	online resource

RDA CORE ELEMENTS AND THE MARC RECORD

The RDA core elements are the required information that must be included in a catalog record. There are specific locations in the MARC record where these core elements are placed. Table 6.2 notes the MARC fields associated with each RDA core element and specific instructions for each area, along with a sample entry.

Table 6.2
RDA Core Elements and MARC Field

MARC Tag	RDA Element	Example	Instructions
	Mode of Issuance	m	A printed resource such as a book is a single unit and designated in the MARC record as a monograph or **m**
020 ISBN 022 ISSN	Identifying Number	1111199999222	Use the ISBN for print, the ISSN for periodicals, or other standard numbers for different media types
100/110	Creator, Relationship Designator	Carroll, Lewis, 1831–1898, author.	This is the principle creator of the work. Use the Library of Congress Name Authorities for authorized name heading. Use tag 110 for corporate name headings. Additional creators can be added using the 700 tag. Include a relationship designator.
245	Title Proper, Other Title Information, Statement of Responsibility	Alice's Adventures through the Looking Glass : And What She Saw / by Lewis Carroll ; Illustrations by John Tenniel.	Transcribe information from the title page or other preferred source of information. Transcribe the title as displayed on the record or use the library's required conventions for capitalization; transcribe the first name listed for the Statement of Responsibility. Do not use Latin abbreviations such as et al.
250	Edition Statement	First edition. [Revised edition]	Transcribe edition information from the title page or other preferred source of information.
264	Place of Publication, Publisher's Name, Publication Date	San Francisco, Calif. : Libraries Unlimited, 2014. New York : Putnam [2015]	Transcribe the information as found on the preferred source of information and use abbreviations for states and countries. Any information that is not listed on the item but is known may be listed in brackets.

Table 6.2 *(Continued)*

MARC Tag	RDA Element	Example	Instructions
300	Extent, Illustrations, Dimensions	x, 150 pages : color illustrations ; 24 cm + maps.	For print items, record preliminary pages in Roman numerals, record numbers of pages, illustrative content, record dimensions in inches or centimeters. Do not abbreviate page numbers but do abbreviate dimensions. Dimensions are not recorded in eBook records. RDA prescribes how specific materials are to be listed. Also record any accompanying materials such as patterns or maps.
336	Content Type	text	Use content types defined by RDA rules. There can be multiple content types in a record.
337	Media Type	unmediated	This is the type of device required to view the material as prescribed by RDA.
338	Carrier Type	volume	This describes how the materials are stored as prescribed by RDA.
490	Series Statement	Alice Adventures Series, no. 5.	If the item is part of the series, include the Title, the number within the series

An important element of the catalog record that is not specified as a core element by RDA include the Notes area, located in the 500s fields of the MARC record, the subject headings, located in the 600s fields of the MARC record, and local call numbers. Important notes to be added to the MARC record may include the following entries:

- 500—General—list general information about the item
- 504—Bibliographic—list information about bibliographies and indexes
- 505—Formatted Contents—list information about the contents such as song titles and table of contents.
- 520—Summary—list a summary of item that would be useful for the patron
- 521—Target Audience—list information about the grade or reading level of the item
- 526—Study Program—list information about the reading or other curricular program associated with the item
- 538—System Details—list information about special software or hardware requirements
- 546—Language—list information about languages associated with the item
- 590—Local—list any information relevant to local needs associated with the item

Table 6.3
Sears **Subject Headings, DDC Call Numbers, and MARC Tags**

MARC Tag		Content		Example
		Local call number		FIC Carroll 2014 092.5 Carroll 2014 B Carroll 2014
504		Bibliographic Note		Includes bibliographical references and index.
520		Summary Note		Alice falls down a rabbit hole and finds an amazing land of wonder.
650		Sears Topical Heading		Rabbits—Fiction.
651		Geographic Heading		England—Fiction.

Subject headings further the finding function of the library catalog and include personal names (600), topical headings (650), geographic headings (651), and local headings (690). Subject headings describing items for the library catalog are identified using authorized subject heading lists such as the *Sears List of Subject Headings* or the *Library of Congress Subject Headings*. To enhance young patrons' ability to find information, school librarians might also find it useful to create a list of local subject headings to use in their cataloging activities.

Table 6.3 shows where subject heading and notes information are listed in the catalog record, along with formatted examples of catalog entries, and additional instructions.

THE CATALOGING MODULE IN THE ILS

Each automated library system includes a cataloging module designed for entering information into a MARC format to create a catalog record. The cataloging module provides several different ways to enter catalog records into the system:

- Records can be imported into the system from another library or vendor.
- Record information can be copied from similar records found in other libraries and pasted into the data entry form.
- The entire record can be created by the cataloger.

Figure 6.1 shows an example of a catalog module that is part of an ILS and the options for creating catalog records they typically provide. Notice the location of the tools within the module for importing records from other libraries, for uploading records from storage devices, and for creating original catalog records in different formats.

STANDARDS AND PROCEDURES FOR COPY CATALOGING

The most common use of the ILS cataloging module by school librarians is for copy cataloging. School librarians engage in a lot of copy cataloging because it is a

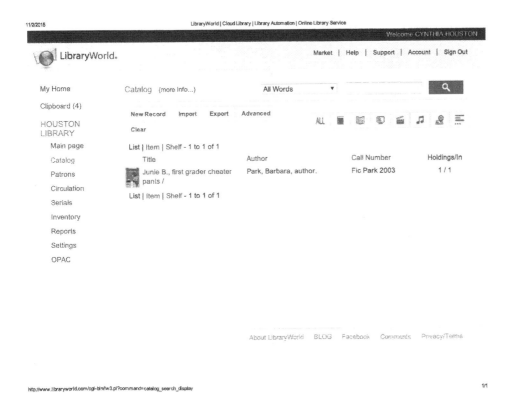

Figure 6.1. ILS catalog module screen

cost-effective way to put new library items into circulation and does not require exten-sive education and training (Fritz, 2011).

Copy cataloging involves importing catalog records into the local system from a source provided by the library's book vendor or from another library. The records are then matched with the information on the local item, edited to comply with RDA stan-dards, and added to the library's OPAC. There is a step-by-step process librarians can follow when importing catalog records into their own systems. Typically, this process involves the following steps:

STEP 1: Locate a record to import—it is usually not difficult to locate and import catalog records into a school library automated catalog. Most ILS catalog modules pro-vide a number of different options for locating and importing catalog records. In the figure of the catalog module screen in the previous section, note the different options for locating records such as an item's title, standard number, and creator, as well as the number of different sources for accessing records including state, national, and inter-national libraries.

STEP 2: Select the record to import—typically, when information for locating records is inserted into the catalog module's search fields, a number of different records are displayed in the search list. The goal here is to find a record that closely matches or is identical to the item being cataloged. Figure 6.2 shows results for a search for *Junie B., First Grader Cheater Pants* by Barbara Park using the item's ISBN number. Notice that two items are retrieved using the OhioLink catalog.

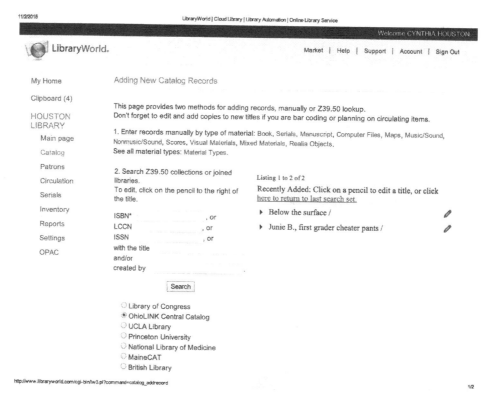

Figure 6.2. Results of catalog record search

STEP 3: View the selected record—in order to select the record that most closely matches the item being cataloged, it is important to carefully review the information in the results list of the catalog search. For example, Figure 6.3 shows one of the retrieved records from the OhioLink catalog. When viewing the record, note not only the information that matches the item to be cataloged, such as the ISBN number, but also the information that must be edited, such as the local call number; RDA core elements such as Content, Media, and Carrier Types; and extent of the item. Because it is important to create the most accurate record as possible, the record should be viewed in MARC format. In this way, every field can be examined and compared with the item being cataloged.

STEP 4: Edit the record to match the item being cataloged—although copy cataloging does save time and effort, it is still important to edit the catalog record so that it matches the item being added to the local library catalog and reflects current cataloging standards and practices. This may mean that changes in a number of MARC fields such as the author, publisher, edition, extent, content type, media type, carrier type, notes, and subject headings should be edited or added to the record. Because later versions of the original items may have changed due to changes in a publisher name or page numbering, older catalog records may not include current information. In other instances, relationship designators must be added to name headings, or abbreviations must be revised to reflect RDA standards. Additionally, records added to school library catalogs should be edited to include *Sears* or local subject headings and curriculum-related

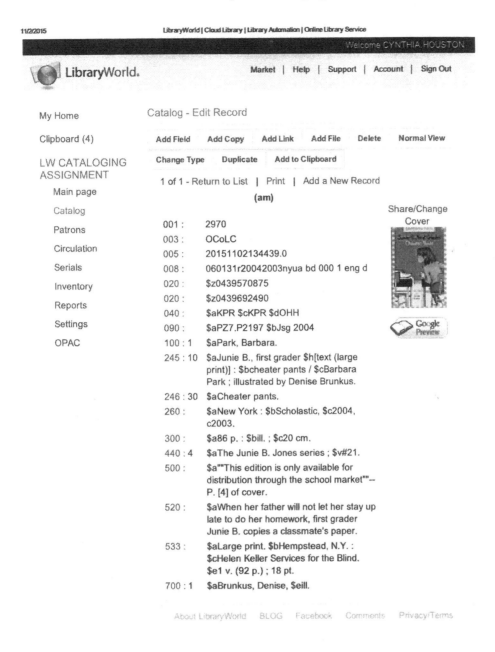

Figure 6.3. Catalog record in MARC format

notes. Figure 6.4 displays the edited version of the catalog record displayed in the previous figure. Note the changes made in the local call number, the author entry field, the publication field, and the extent field.

STEP 5: Save the record—in many cataloging modules, changes to records are not automatically saved, making this a separate but very important step in the copy cataloging process. No one wants to have gone through the tedious process of editing a catalog record to find that changes have not been saved in the system.

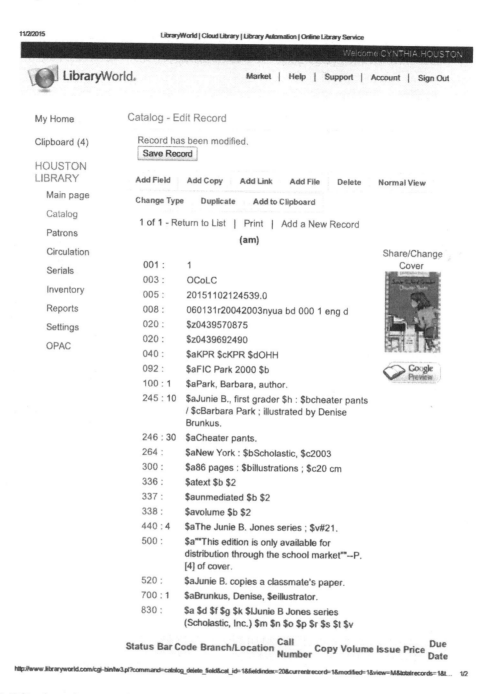

Figure 6.4. Edited catalog record in MARC format

STEP 6: Add the record to the OPAC by adding a local call number and other required local information—records are not automatically added to the local catalog and made public to catalog users. In most automated catalogs, adding an item to the local OPAC requires additional steps such as adding a local call number. Figure 6.5 shows an example screen for adding a record to the catalog. Note the fields for catalogers to add information about the location of the items, bar code number, price, and information required for inventory activities.

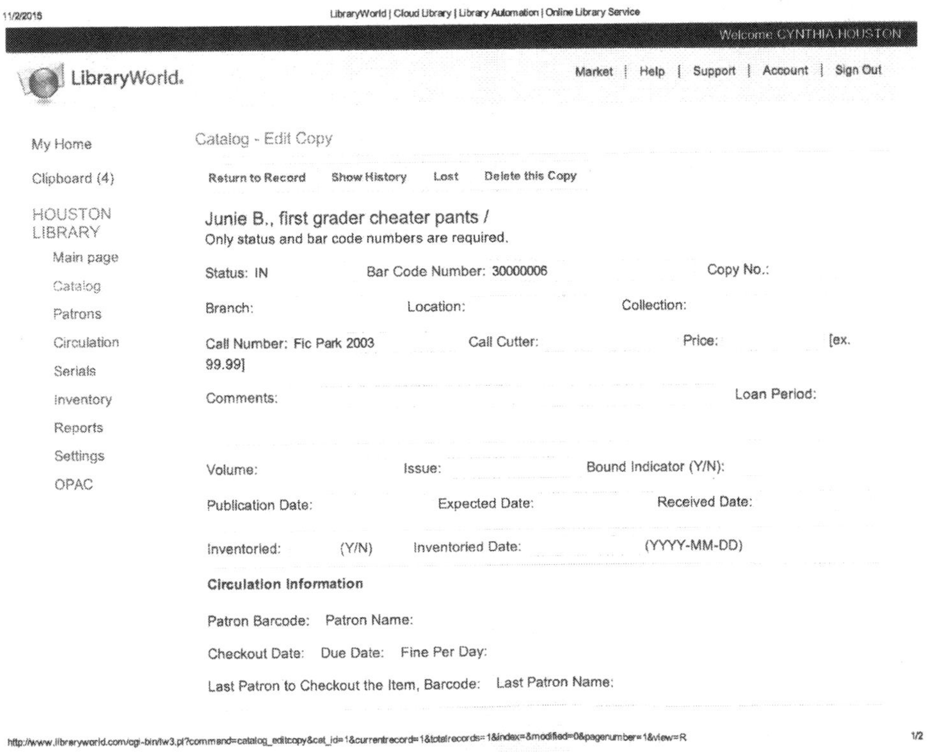

Figure 6.5. Catalog utility for adding records to the OPAC

STEP 7: Search for the record in the OPAC and review for accuracy—to ensure that catalog records have been correctly edited and added to the OPAC, it is important to carry out the final step of searching for the item in the library catalog. To do this, catalogers must exit the cataloging module and search for the item by name or ISBN number in the local library OPAC. If the record appears, then it has been successfully added to the catalog. At this point, it is also a good time to review the information for accuracy one more time before moving on to cataloging the next item. Figure 6.6 shows the OPAC display of the edited catalog record.

STANDARDS AND PROCEDURES FOR ORIGINAL CATALOGING

In the event that the vendor does not supply the MARC record and the record is not available from any other source, a school librarian must create an original catalog record by entering the information manually into the ILS catalog module. If the item is a book, much of this information can be copied from the Library of Congress CIP information on the inside or verso page of the item. When doing this, it is important to follow professional standards for descriptive cataloging and subject analysis to ensure that the record in the catalog is accurate and meets professional standards (Intner & Weihs, 2015). Typically, there are two views available for entering data into a catalog record, the MARC view and the labeled field view. Figure 6.7 shows a typical MARC view in a cataloging module. Most catalogers choose the MARC view for original cataloging in order to make sure they are including accurate information in the appropriate MARC fields. When using the MARC view, there is a data field for every MARC tag required for the item as well as subfields that describe specific information about the item.

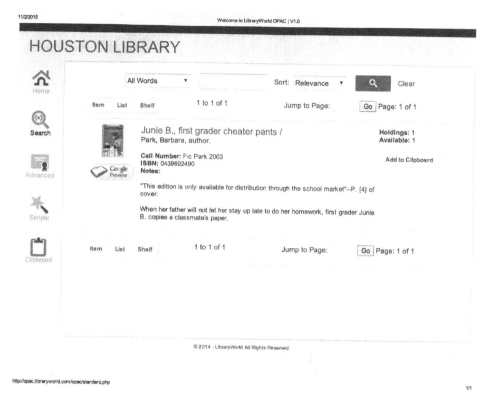80   Organizing Information in School Libraries

Figure 6.6. Edited catalog record in OPAC file

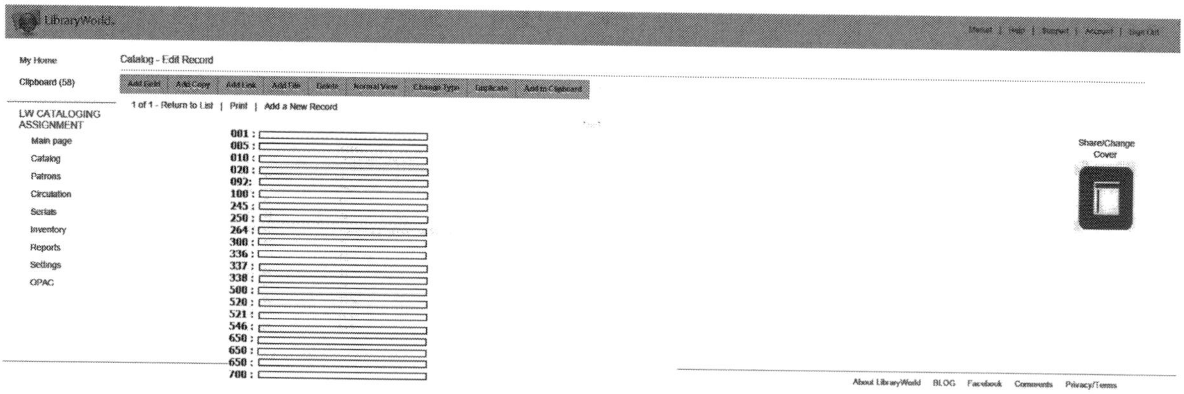

Figure 6.7. Catalog record MARC view

When first beginning to create original records, Jacox et al. (2014) recommend breaking the cataloging task into stages that include identifying what is being cataloged, identifying information that is to be transcribed and recorded, and identifying appropriate subject headings and call number for the item. These stages describe the step-by-step process catalogers go through in creating catalog records. This process is often referred to as the "workflow," because it outlines a path for accomplishing the cataloging task in a systematic manner and ensures that all the requirements and standards are satisfied. The following is a suggested workflow for cataloging an original record.

STEP 1: Identify what is being cataloged and enter information about:

- Mode of issuance—identify the form the item takes using RDA terminology.
- Content type—identify the means through which the content is communicated using RDA terminology.
- Media type—identify the means through which the content is displayed using RDA terminology.
- Carrier type—identify the means by which the content is transmitted or contained using RDA terminology.
- Preferred source of information—identify the location of the information used for cataloging on the item itself.

STEP 2: Identify information displayed on the item to be transcribed and the format for each entry:

- Title—identify the title on the preferred source of information.
- Statement of responsibility—identify the creators listed on the preferred source of information; transcribe this information into the catalog record.
- Creators/contributors—identify all the creators and contributors involved in the work; transcribe this information into the catalog record.
- Publication information—identify the publisher, location of publication, and date on the preferred source of information; transcribe this information into the catalog record.
- Edition information—identify the edition information on the preferred source of information; transcribe this information into the catalog record.
- Series title (if applicable)—identify the series information on the preferred source of information; transcribe this information into the catalog record.
- Identifier for manifestation—identify the standard number for the item and enter it in the catalog record.

STEP 3: Identify information to be recorded and the format for each entry:

- Extent of the item—identify the extent, illustrative content, and dimensions of the item; use ISBD punctuation.
- Notes—include summary notes, formatted content notes, language notes, system notes, or any other relevant notes in the catalog record.

STEP 4: Apply subject headings and call numbers:

- Subject headings—identify *Sears* main subject heading and associated DDC (for nonfiction titles).
- Call number—add Dewey classification, author name, and publication date as necessary to build a call number.

STEP 5: Add the item to the catalog and review the entry in the OPAC:

- Add the record—use the cataloging module tools to add the record to the library catalog.
- Review the record—exit the catalog module; use the OPAC to locate the record and review for accuracy.

Alice's Adventures in Wonderland

by Lewis Carroll

Philadelphia, Altemus

1895

Illustrations by John Tenniel

Notes: This book has 200 pages, with color illustrati
is 10 cm in length
The LCCN number is 02020394
Lewis Carroll was born in 1832 and died in 1898
The illustrator was born in 1820 and died in 1914

Figure 6.8. Print item example record

PUTTING IT ALL TOGETHER: RDA AND MARC

For school librarians who do not regularly catalog items for their library, applying RDA rules, locating subject headings, and building call numbers might appear to be a daunting task. However, like many skills and procedures, these activities become easier with practice. The following is an example of a catalog record with a description of the workflow and notes about special considerations for each entry. By following this example, beginning catalogers can review and understand the cataloging process and have an example to follow as they create original records on their own.

Example 1
Print Item Example Record and Workflow

Workflow	RDA Element	
STEP 1: Identify what is being cataloged and enter information	Mode of issuance, Content type, Media type, Carrier type, Preferred source of information	
STEP 2: Identify information displayed on the item to be transcribed	Title, Statement of responsibility, Creators, Contributors, Publication information, Edition information, Series title (if applicable) Identifier for manifestation	
STEP 3: Identify information to be recorded	Creator entry, Extent of the item, Illustrative content, Dimensions, Notes, Language	
STEP 4: Apply Subject Headings and Call Numbers	Identify Sears main subject heading and DDC (for nonfiction titles); Add Author name and publication date as necessary to build a call number; Add the item to the catalog	

MARC tag	RDA Element	Field Entry
	Mode of issuance	m
	Local call number	FIC Carroll 1895
010	Identifying Number	0202–0394
100	Creator, Relationship Designator	Carroll, Lewis, 1832–1898, author.
245	Title Proper, Other Title Information, Statement of Responsibility	Alice's Adventures in Wonderland / by Lewis Carroll ; Illustrations by John Tenniel.
264	Place of Publication, Publisher's Name, Publication Date	Philadelphia, Pa. : Altemus, 1895.
300	Extent, Illustrations, Dimensions	200 pages : color illustrations ; 10 cm
336	Content Type	text
336	Content Type	still image
337	Media Type	unmediated
338	Carrier Type	volume
650	Sears Topical Heading	Rabbits—Fiction.
655	Genre Heading	Fantasy fiction.
700	Personal name added entry	Tenniel, John, 1820–1914, illustrator.

INTERNET RESOURCES

Resource Description and Access Toolkit: http://access.rdatoolkit.org/
Official website for RDA Rules

Library of Congress Authorities: http://authorities.loc.gov/
Authorized name headings

MARC Standards: http://www.loc.gov/marc/
MARC 21 Standards from the Library of Congress

Bibliographic Formats and Standards: http://www.oclc.org/bibformats/en.html
OCLC Standards for MARC records

Classify: An experimental classification web service: http://classify.oclc.org/classify2/
Find Dewey classifications by titles, ISBN numbers, or subjects

EXERCISES

1. Use the following worksheets to complete a record for three print items of your choice. In your reflection, note the tasks you found difficult to accomplish and tasks you found easy to do.

Table 6.4
Cataloging Worksheets

MARC	RDA Element	Field Entry	Reflection
	Mode of issuance		
	Local call number		
010/020	Identifying Number		
100	Creator, Relationship Designator		
245	Title Proper, Other Title Information, Statement of Responsibility		
250	Edition Statement		
264	Place of Publication, Publisher's Name, Publication Date		
300	Extent, Illustrations, Dimensions		
336	Content Type		
337	Media Type		
338	Carrier Type		
490 830	Series Statement Series Uniform Title		
504	Bibliography Note		
650	Sears Topical Heading		
690	Local Subject Heading		

Table 6.4 *(Continued)*

MARC	RDA Element	Field Entry	Reflection
	Mode of issuance		
	Local call number		
010/020	Identifying Number		
100	Creator, Relationship Designator		
245	Title Proper, Other Title Information, Statement of Responsibility		
250	Edition Statement		
264	Place of Publication, Publisher's Name, Publication Date		
300	Extent, Illustrations, Dimensions		
336	Content Type		
337	Media Type		
338	Carrier Type		
490 830	Series Statement Series Uniform Title		
504	Bibliography Note		
650	Sears Topical Heading		
690	Local Subject Heading		

MARC	RDA Element	Field Entry	Reflection
	Mode of issuance		
	Local call number		
010/020	Identifying Number		
100	Creator, Relationship Designator		
245	Title Proper, Other Title Information, Statement of Responsibility		
250	Edition Statement		
264	Place of Publication, Publisher's Name, Publication Date		
300	Extent, Illustrations, Dimensions		
336	Content Type		
337	Media Type		
338	Carrier Type		
490 830	Series Statement Series Uniform Title		
504	Bibliography Note		
650	Sears Topical Heading		
690	Local Subject Heading		

2. Use an online catalog such as WorldCat to locate and review a catalog record of an item with the ISBN number 9780141197302. Create a MARC worksheet and enter information into each field using RDA rules.

Table 6.5
Cataloging Worksheet for ISBN 9780141197302

MARC	RDA Element	Field Entry
	Mode of issuance	
	Local call number	
020	Identifying Number	
100	Creator, Relationship Designator	
245	Title Proper, Other Title Information, Statement of Responsibility	
264	Place of Publication, Publisher's Name, Publication Date	
300	Extent, Illustrations, Dimensions	
336	Content Type	
337	Media Type	
337	Media Type	
338	Carrier Type	
650	Sears Topical Heading	
650	Sears Topical Heading	

7

Cataloging Print Resources

INTRODUCTION

The print collection in the school library comprises the majority of the library's holdings and continues to be the most widely used service the library provides. Maintaining a current collection of fiction and nonfiction titles is an essential function of the library. Because new items are added to the collection all the time, making sure that print items such as books and magazines are cataloged quickly and correctly might pose a challenging task for the school librarian; but with some cataloging practice and an efficient workflow, this challenge can be met with a minimum of difficulty.

CATALOGING PRINT MATERIALS

Before beginning the cataloging task, think about the item, its relation to the collection, and the users of that collection. This will help connect the cataloging workflow to the overall mission of the library and ensure that users locate and access information (Karpuk, 2008). Print resources that are typically added to the school library catalog include fiction materials that support the school literacy program and nonfiction materials that support the school curriculum. Other print materials might include periodicals that support the curriculum or interests of library users. The workflow for cataloging these items follows a process discussed in previous chapters with specific procedures for cataloging print materials. The process begins with creating the MARC record either on a print worksheet or in the ILS cataloging module using the workflow process discussed in Chapter 6. When the process is complete, the last step is to review the entry in the OPAC. The workflow for print materials is outlined in the following section. The remainder of the chapter contains five completed catalog records and five practice catalog records with answers located in the Appendix. To gain practice in cataloging print materials, examine the completed records and use them as a model to complete the five remaining practice records. The RDA Summary Sheet located in the Appendix provides assistances with applying RDA standards and ISBD punctuation to the appropriate areas of the MARC record. An excellent resource for additional cataloging examples is the second edition of *Unlocking the Mysteries of Cataloging: A Workbook of Examples* (Haynes, Fountain, & Zwierski, 2015).

WORKFLOW FOR PRINT RESOURCES

STEP 1: Identify what is being cataloged and enter information about the following:

- Preferred source of information—RDA standards have designated the title page of printed items to be the preferred source of information, so this is the first place a cataloger looks for information. Additional publication information is typically located in the CIP information on the verso page. Most of the information required for completing catalog records for printed items will be found on these sources of information.

- Mode of issuance—mode of issuance for most print materials will be a "single unit" if they are books and "multipart monographs" for multivolume resources such as encyclopedias. In both cases, the MARC notation on the LDR/07 area of the record is the letter **m** for books or monographs. Materials that are considered "serials" such as magazines use the letter **s**. This information is generally added to the record automatically when using an ILS cataloging module and selecting a format for the item being cataloged.

EXAMPLE: LDR/07   m

- Content type—printed materials are limited in their content type and therefore only contain printed words or "text," and photos or illustrations, referred to as "still image." The MARC tag for Content type is 336.

EXAMPLE: 336   text

- Media type—because print items do not require any device for viewing or accessing information, they are listed as "unmediated." The MARC tag for Media type is 337.

EXAMPLE: 337   unmediated

- Carrier type—virtually all printed items are bound via staples, stitching, or glue, and therefore are listed as a "volume." The MARC tag for Carrier type is 338.

EXAMPLE: 338   volume

STEP 2: Identify information displayed on the item to be transcribed:

- Title—RDA standards require title information to be transcribed from the preferred source of information. Use ISBD punctuation to transcribe the title information into the Title and Statement of Responsibility area of the 245 MARC record field. Different libraries have different procedures for transcribing title information from the item into the catalog record. Some libraries transcribe

the information as it appears on the item, while other libraries follow specific
rules for capitalization.

- Statement of responsibility—RDA standards require the statement of
responsibility information to be transcribed from the chief source of information. Different libraries have different procedures for transcribing information from the item into the catalog record. Some libraries transcribe the
information as it appears on the item, while other libraries follow specific
rules for capitalization. Some libraries list all the creators and contributors
listed on the preferred source of information, while others shorten this list.
Use ISBD punctuation to transcribe the statement of responsibility information into the Title and Statement of Responsibility area of the 245 MARC
record field.

  EXAMPLE: 245   The Black Cat Came Back : Good Luck Poems by Cats /
    written by Persia Siamese ; illustrations by Tabby Calico.

- Creators—RDA standards require that creator information be included in the
record as a core element. Use the Library of Congress Name Authority headings to locate authorized name headings, as well as birth and death dates. The
relationship designator associated with books is typically "author." The 100
MARC record field is used for individual authors; the 110 field is used for a
corporate name.

  EXAMPLE: 100   Siamese, Persia, 1959-, author.

- Contributors—RDA standards require that contributors and their relationships such as "author" or "illustrator" be included in a catalog record. Use the
Library of Congress Name Authorities to locate authorized name headings,
as well as birth and death dates. Contributors other than the main author are
added to the record in the 700 MARC field if the contributor is a person, or the
710 field if it is a corporate entity.

  EXAMPLE: 700   Calico, Tabby, 1974-, illustrator.

- Publication information—RDA standards require that information about the
publication, manufacture, distribution, or copyright of an item be included
in the catalog record, as well as the location and date of this event. Use ISBD
punctuation to list the location of the publisher, the publisher name, and date
of publication. If there is a copyright date and no publication date, list the
date in brackets and add another 264 field to list the copyright date with copyright symbol. Transcribe the publication location from the preferred source of
information.
  Transcribe the publisher name from the preferred source of information. This
information is listed in the 264 MARC field.

EXAMPLE: 264   Westport, Conn. : Sweet on Cats Press, 2015.
EXAMPLE: 264   Westport, Conn. : Sweet on Cats Press, [2015]
           264   ©2015

- Edition information—edition information is often but not always listed on books and rarely listed on magazines unless they are special editions. Transcribe edition information from the preferred source of information into the 250 MARC field.

EXAMPLE: 250   Second Edition.

- Series title—books that are part of a series will often have a series title listed on the preferred source of information. Transcribe this information from the preferred source of information into the 490 MARC field using ISBD punctuation. This information also must be included in an 8XX MARC field as an added entry; in this example, the added entry is to denote the Uniform Title of the series.

EXAMPLE: 490   Sweet on Cats Poetry ; vol. 2
EXAMPLE: 830   Sweet on Cats Poetry Series.

- Identifier for manifestation—standard numbers associated with print materials are typically ISBN numbers for books or ISSN numbers for serials. Use the 13-number ISBN when it is available and remove the hyphens when entering this information in the 020 MARC field. If the item is a serial with an ISSN number, do not remove the hyphens and use the 022 MARC field.

EXAMPLE: 020   9789070002343

STEP 3: Identify information to be recorded.

- Extent—RDA requires that the extent of the item, along with its illustrative content and dimensions, be included in the record. In the 300 MARC field, record this information using ISBD punctuation from an examination of the item's page numbers, preliminary pages, illustrations, and measurements. Do not abbreviate any words except for the length of the books, which is measured in centimeters. Use Roman numerals for numbering preliminary pages. Use the term "illustrations" if there are only black-and-white illustrations and "color illustrations" if they are in color.

EXAMPLE: 300   iv, 417 pages : color illustrations ; 22 cm

- Notes—although not an RDA-required core element, notes do provide essential information about an item and are useful to users as they search the library catalog for information. Typical notes that are part of catalog records for books include general notes located in the 500 MARC field, formatted contents notes located in the 505 MARC field, summary notes located in the 520 MARC field, target audience notes in the 521 field, study program notes in the 526 field, and language notes located in the 546 field. Summary information may be taken from the book jacket or summary of contents; bibliographic information generally includes information about the item's references and index; target audience notes refer to the age group the item is written for; and study program notes contain curriculum information.

EXAMPLE: 520   An adventure story featuring a teen sleuth and a wild treasure hunt.

STEP 4: Apply subject headings, classification, and call numbers.

- Subject headings—use the *Sears Subject Headings* list to identify the main heading for the item, along with other appropriate headings and subdivisions. Omit the subdivision "Juvenile literature" from all headings. Add local subject headings if necessary to facilitate searching. Use the 600 MARC field for name headings, 650 for topical subject headings, and the 651 for geographic subject headings.

EXAMPLE: 650   Cats—Poetry.

STEP 5: Add the item to the catalog and review the entry.

- Classification—use the *Sears Subject Headings* and *Abridged Dewey Decimal Classification* to determine the item's classification. Incorporate the classification into the call number for nonfiction items and collected works of literature.
- Call number—use the local library call number notation system for fiction and nonfiction titles. Often, magazines and other periodicals will use a special notation to indicate that they are shelved in a separate section of the library. This information is typically added to the record when the item is added to the library catalog.

INTERNET RESOURCES

Resource Description and Access Toolkit: http://access.rdatoolkit.org/
Official website for RDA Rules

Library of Congress Authorities: http://authorities.loc.gov/
Authorized name headings

MARC Standards: http://www.loc.gov/marc/
MARC 21 Standards from the Library of Congress

Bibliographic Formats and Standards: http://www.oclc.org/bibformats/en.html
OCLC Standards for MARC records

Classify: An experimental classification web service: http://classify.oclc.org/classify2/
Find Dewey classifications by titles, ISBN numbers, or subjects

EXERCISES

Example 1
Print Item Practice Exercise

The Black Cat Came Back:
Good Luck Poems by Cats
written by Persia Siamese
illustrations by Tabby Calico
Second Revised Edition

Sweet on Cats Press - Westport
Connecticut - 2015

Notes: This 21x 26 cm book has 4 preliminary pages, 125 pages, black and white illustrations and an index; the author was born in 1959. This is an Accelerated Reader Program Book.
ISBN 978-1-11828-817-1

Summary: Do you ever wonder what cats are saying? Acutally they are reciting poetry to each other based on their nine lives. The author and illustrator of this unusual collection will delight young audiences with adventure poems from their favorite pets.

MARC Tag	RDA Element	Field Entry
	Mode of issuance	m
	Local call number	808.6 Siamese 2015
020	Identifying Number	9781118288171
100	Creator, Relationship Designator	Siamese, Persia, 1959-, author.
245	Title Proper, Other Title Information, Statement of Responsibility	The Black Cat Came Back : Good Luck Poems by Cats / written by Persia Siamese ; illustrations by Tabby Calico.
250	Edition Statement	Second Revised Edition.
264	Place of Publication, Publisher's Name, Publication Date	Westport, Connecticut : Sweet on Cats Press, 2015.
300	Extent, Illustrations, Dimensions	iv, 125 pages : illustrations ; 26 cm
336	Content Type	text
336	Content Type	still image
337	Media Type	unmediated
338	Carrier Type	volume
500	General Note	Includes index.
520	Summary Note	Do you ever wonder what cats are saying? Actually, they are reciting poetry to each other based on their nine lives. The author and illustrator of this unusual collection will delight young audiences with adventure poems from their favorite pets.
526	Study Program Note	Accelerated Reader.
650	Sears Topical Heading	Cats—Literary collections. Cats—Poetry.
700	Name added entry	Calico, Tabby, illustrator.

Example 2
Print Item Practice Exercise

It came from the TV:
Stories from Cyberspace

by Fester Fogg and Gamma Ray Jones

Penguin - New York
First Edition
1955

Notes: This 18 x 23 cm book has 275 pages, color illustrations a bibliography and index; the author was born in 1935 and died in 1990. This is a Reading Counts program book.
ISBN 978-1-61828-877-4

Summary: Noted science fiction writers Fester Fogg and Gamma Ray Jones create seven delightful short stories that include televisions, zombies, and middle grades students.

MARC Tag	RDA Element	Field Entry
	Mode of issuance	m
	Local call number	808.3 Fogg 1955
020	Identifying Number	9781618288774
100	Creator, Relationship Designator	Fogg, Fester, 1935–1990, author.
245	Title Proper, Other Title Information, Statement of Responsibility	It came from the TV : Stories from Cyberspace / by Fester Fogg and Gamma Ray Jones.
250	Edition Statement	First Edition.
264	Place of Publication, Publisher's Name, Publication Date	New York : Penguin, 1955.
300	Extent, Illustrations, Dimensions	275 pages : color illustrations ; 23 cm
336	Content Type	text
336	Content Type	still image
337	Media Type	unmediated
338	Carrier Type	volume
504	Bibliographic/Supplementary Content Note	Includes bibliographical references and index.
520	Summary Note	Noted science fiction writers Fester Fogg and Gamma Ray Jones create seven delightful short stories that include televisions, zombies, and middle grade students.
526	Study Program Note	Reading Counts.
650	Sears Topical Heading	Science fiction—Literary collections.
700	Name added entry	Jones, Gamma Ray, author.

Example 3
Print Item Practice Exercise

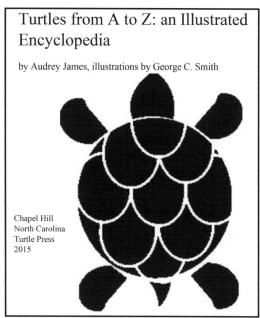

Turtles from A to Z: an Illustrated
Encyclopedia

by Audrey James, illustrations by George C. Smith

Chapel Hill
North Carolina
Turtle Press
2015

Notes: This 17 x 25 cm book has 17 preliminary pages 300 pages, colored illustrations a bibliography and index; the author was born in 1986. The illustrator was born in 1972. This is an elementary grade level resource. ISBN 978-5-61648-897-1

Summary: U.S. turtle experts join forces to create the defninitive guide to American turtles for young naturalists.

MARC Tag	RDA Element	Field Entry
	Mode of issuance	m
	Call number	579.92 James 2015
020	Identifying Number	9785616488971
100	Creator, Relationship Designator	James, Audrey, 1986-, author.
245	Title Proper, Other Title Information, Statement of Responsibility	Turtles from A to Z : an Illustrated Encyclopedia / by Audrey James ; illustrations by George C. Smith.
264	Place of Publication, Publisher's Name, Publication Date	Chapel Hill, North Carolina : Turtle Press, 2015.
300	Extent, Illustrations, Dimensions	xvii, 300 pages : color illustrations ; 25 cm
336	Content Type	text
336	Content Type	still image
337	Media Type	unmediated
338	Carrier Type	volume
504	Bibliographic/Supplementary Content Note	Includes bibliographical references and index.
520	Summary Note	U.S. turtle experts join forces to create the definitive guide to American turtles for young naturalists.
521	Target Audience	Elementary grade level
650	Sears Topical Heading	Turtles—Encyclopedias.
700	Name added entry	Smith, George C., 1972-, illustrator.

Example 4
Print Item Practice Exercise

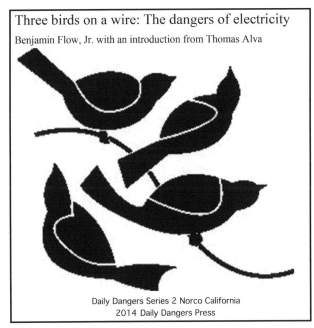

Three birds on a wire: The dangers of electricity

Benjamin Flow, Jr. with an introduction from Thomas Alva

Daily Dangers Series 2 Norco California
2014 Daily Dangers Press

Notes: This 15 x 22 cm book has 4 preliminary pages 300 pages, illustrations, and index; The author was born in 1980. ISBN 948-3-61848-572-2

Summary: Electricity is all around us and we forget the dangers lurking in faulty outlets and electrical wiring. This book helps children understand the dangers of electricity and how to avoid accidents.

MARC Tag	RDA Element	Field Entry
	Mode of issuance	m
	Call number	363.1 Flow 2014
020	Identifying Number	9483618485772
100	Creator, Relationship Designator	Flow, Benjamin, Jr., 1980-, author.
245	Title Proper, Other Title Information, Statement of Responsibility	Three birds on a wire : The dangers of electricity / Benjamin Flow, Jr. ; with an introduction from Thomas Alva.
264	Place of Publication, Publisher's Name, Publication Date	Norco, California : Daily Dangers Press, 2014.
300	Extent, Illustrations, Dimensions	iv, 300 pages : illustrations ; 22 cm
336	Content Type	text
336	Content Type	still image
337	Media Type	unmediated
338	Carrier Type	volume
490	Series Statement	Daily Dangers Series ; 2
500	General Note	Includes index.
520	Summary Note	Electricity is all around us, and we forget the dangers lurking in faulty outlets and electrical wiring. This book helps children understand the dangers of electricity and how to avoid accidents.
650	Sears Topical Heading	Accidents—Prevention. Electricity—Accidents. Home accidents.
830	Series Added Entry Uniform Title	Daily Dangers Series ; 2.

Example 5
Print Item Practice Exercise

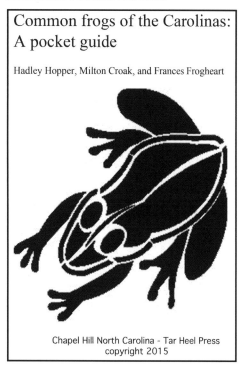

Common frogs of the Carolinas:
A pocket guide

Hadley Hopper, Milton Croak, and Frances Frogheart

Chapel Hill North Carolina - Tar Heel Press
copyright 2015

Notes: This 10 x 15 cm book has 16 preliminary pages 350 pages, color illustrations, bibliography and index; the author was born in 1975 and died in 2014. ISBN 971-3-61648-407-1

Summary: For frog experts and novices alike, this is a pocket guide to native and foreign frog species commonly found in the Carolina waterways. The guide provides information about species, mating habits, and habitats.

MARC Tag	RDA Element	Field Entry
	Mode of issuance	m
	Local call number	597.8 Hopper 2015
020	Identifying Number	9713616484071
100	Creator, Relationship Designator	Hopper, Hadley, 1975–2014, author.
245	Title Proper, Other Title Information, Statement of Responsibility	Common frogs of the Carolinas : A pocket guide / Hadley Hopper, Milton Croak, and Frances Frogheart.
264	Place of Publication, Publisher's Name, Publication Date	Chapel Hill, North Carolina : Tar Heel Press, [2015]
264	Copyright Date	©2015
300	Extent, Illustrations, Dimensions	xvi, 350 pages : color illustrations ; 15 cm
336	Content Type	text
336	Content Type	still image
337	Media Type	unmediated
338	Carrier Type	volume
504	Bibliographic, Supplementary Content Note	Includes bibliographical references and index.
520	Summary Note	For frog experts and novices alike, this is a pocket guide to native and foreign frog species commonly found in the Carolina waterways. The guide provides information about species, mating habits, and habitats.
650	Sears Topical Heading	Frogs—Southern States—Guidebooks.
700	Name added entry	Croak, Milton, author.
700	Name added entry	Frogheart, Frances, author.

Example 6
Print Item Practice Exercise

COFFEE! Our Favorite Addiction

by Janet Jitters

Seattle Washington - Starbarks and Sons publishers
Common Addictions Series v.4
4th edition
2015

Notes: This 15 x 23 cm book has 200 pages, and bibliograpnic references; the author was born in 1975.
ISBN 941-3-81638-457-1

Summary: Many of us cannot go a day without our morning cup of Joe, but we never consider the health effects of caffeine addiction. This book describes the process by which we become addicted to coffee and the side effects of this habit.

MARC Tag	RDA Element	Field Entry
	Mode of issuance	
	Local call number	
020	Identifying Number	
100/110	Creator, Relationship Designator	
245	Title Proper, Other Title Information, Statement of Responsibility	
250	Edition Statement	
264	Place of Publication, Publisher's Name, Publication Date	
300	Extent, Illustrations, Dimensions	
336	Content Type	
337	Media Type	
338	Carrier Type	
490	Series Statement	
520	Summary Note	
504	Bibliographic/Supplementary Content Note	
650	Sears Topical Heading	
690	Local Topical Heading	
830	Series Added Entry Uniform Title	

Example 7
Print Item Practice Exercise

Runaway Librarian: A Marion
Librarian Mystery

Joan James with
Dilbert Slathers

Limited Libraries
New York - 2013

Notes: This 15 x 23 cm book has 250 pages; the author was born in 1986.
ISBN 981-3-51638-407-2

Summary: Join Marion Librarian on her motor scooter mystery tour of the English countryside. This story features a visit to Downtown Abbey where she solves the murder of Mr. Green Jeans.

MARC Tag	RDA Element	Field Entry
	Mode of issuance	
	Local call number	
020	Identifying Number	
100	Creator, Relationship Designator	
245	Title Proper, Other Title Information, Statement of Responsibility	
264	Place of Publication, Publisher's Name, Publication Date	
300	Extent, Illustrations, Dimensions	
336	Content Type	
337	Media Type	
338	Carrier Type	
490	Series Statement	
520	Summary Note	
650	Sears Topical Heading	
651	Geographic Heading	
700	Name added entry	
830	Series Added Entry Uniform Title	

Example 8
Print Item Practice Exercise

The Kracken Myth: Large Underwater Sea Creatures and their Mythological Origins

Oliver Calimari and Sidney Squidler with illustrations by Inkver Fisk
3rd. revised edition

The strange and terrifying sea series vol.2
Bangor - Maine - Calimari Bros. Press
2014

Note: This 18 x 26 cm book has 4 preliminary pages, black and white illustrations, 250 pages, with bibliographic references and index; the author was born in 1972.
ISBN 941-8-51733-607-2

Summary: Legends abound about the sea monsters inhabiting our deep oceans. The authors of this book link mythical sea monsters such as krackens with large sea life recently discovered on deep ocean dives.

MARC Tag	RDA Element	Field Entry
	Mode of issuance	
	Local call number	
020	Identifying Number	
100	Creator, Relationship Designator	
245	Title Proper, Other Title Information, Statement of Responsibility	
250	Edition Statement	
264	Place of Publication, Publisher's Name, Publication Date	
300	Extent, Illustrations, Dimensions	
336	Content Type	
336	Content Type	
337	Media Type	
338	Carrier Type	
490	Series Statement	
504	Bibliographic/Supplementary Content Note	
520	Summary Note	
650	Sears Topical Heading	
700	Name added entry	
700	Name added entry	
830	Series Added Entry Uniform Title	

Example 9
Print Item Practice Exercise

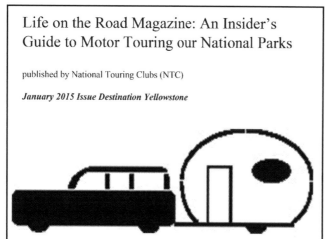

Life on the Road Magazine: An Insider's
Guide to Motor Touring our National Parks

published by National Touring Clubs (NTC)

January 2015 Issue Destination Yellowstone

Notes: This 16 x 27 cm magazine has 250 pages, color
photograpns, maps, and bibliographic references. The magazine
is published in Las Vegas, Nevada, but this is not on the item.
LCCN 2571-8034

Summary: The January 2015 issue focuses on winter touring at
Yellowstone National Park.

MARC Tag	RDA Element	Field Entry
	Mode of issuance	
	Local call number	
022	Identifying Number	
245	Title Proper, Other Title Information, Statement of Responsibility	
264	Place of Publication, Publisher's Name, Publication Date	
300	Extent, Illustrations, Dimensions	
336	Content Type	
336	Content Type	
337	Media Type	
338	Carrier Type	
490	Series Statement	
520	Summary Note	
504	Bibliographic/Supplementary Content Note	
650	Sears Topical Heading	
830	Series Added Entry Uniform Title	

Example 10
Print Item Practice Exercise

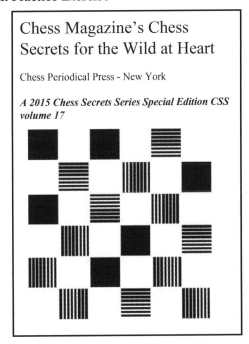

Chess Magazine's Chess
Secrets for the Wild at Heart

Chess Periodical Press - New York

A 2015 Chess Secrets Series Special Edition CSS
volume 17

This 7 x 9 cm book has 50 pages and illustrations.
LCCN 2771-6534

Summary: Use chess masters' "Wild at Heart"
strategies to win your next timed chess matches.

MARC Tag	RDA Element	Field Entry
	Mode of issuance	
	Local call number	
022	Identifying Number	
245	Title Proper, Other Title Information, Statement of Responsibility	
264	Place of Publication, Publisher's Name, Publication Date	
300	Extent, Illustrations, Dimensions	
336	Content Type	
336	Content Type	
337	Media Type	
338	Carrier Type	
490	Series Statement	
520	Summary Note	
650	Sears Topical Heading	
710	Corporate Author Added Entry	
830	Series Added Entry Uniform Title	

8

Cataloging Picture Books, Graphic Novels, Audiovisual, and Realia Resources

INTRODUCTION

Picture books for early readers and graphic novels for young adults are always a part of the school library's holdings and often among the most widely circulated materials. Although audiovisual media are also available online, current audiovisual items a school library holds almost always include music CDs, videos in DVD or Blu-ray format, audio books on CD or Playaway format, and possibly record albums, cassettes, and video tapes. Non-print collections housed in the library may include a variety of items including board games, models, and kits. Maintaining a current collection of picture books, graphic novels, audiovisual titles, and non-print resources is an essential function of the library because they provide a wealth of information resources in multimedia formats. Making sure that these items are cataloged is a task for librarians because these types of catalog records contain a great deal of more descriptive information than print materials, but with some cataloging practice and an efficient workflow process, this challenge can be met and items can move quickly from the cataloging cart to the library shelves.

WORKFLOW FOR ILLUSTRATED, AUDIOVISUAL, AND REALIA MATERIALS

Picture books, graphic novels, audiovisual, and non-print resources typically added to the school library catalog include curriculum-related materials in all subject areas, be they adaptations of literary works, science programs, models, or educational games. The workflow for cataloging items follows the process discussed in previous chapters, with special procedures for cataloging resources in different formats. The workflow process is outlined in the following text. The remainder of the chapter contains five completed catalog records and five practice catalog records with answers located in the Appendix. To gain practice in cataloging these types of materials, examine the completed records and use them as a model to complete the five remaining records. Use the RDA Summary Sheet located in the Appendix of this book to assist with applying RDA standards, ISBD punctuation, and the appropriate MARC fields to the records.

STEP 1: Identify what is being cataloged and enter information about:

• Preferred source of information—RDA rules have designated the title page of printed media, the title screen of visual media, and the cover of audio and realia items to be the preferred sources of information. Additional publication information is typically located on the verso page of print items and the label of audiovisual items.

• Mode of issuance—the mode of issuance for picture books, graphic novels, and most audiovisual and non-print materials will be a single unit. The MARC notation in the LDR/07 area of the record is the letter **m** for "monograph." This information is often recorded automatically in the MARC record when using the cataloging module of an ILS.

• Content type—the content type for picture books and graphic novels is the same for illustrated printed materials and will most likely include "text" and "still image." Audiovisual and non-print materials have more content types than printed materials. Generally, any movie or television program is listed as a "two-dimensional moving image" but may also contain "still image" if there are photographs, "spoken word" if there is narration, or "performed music" if the item features musical performances. Audio books contain primarily "spoken word," while music CDs contain "performed music." The Content type for non-print materials such as models, kits, and games is typically "three-dimensional form." The RDA Summary Sheet in the Appendix of this book will assist with identifying the appropriate content types. The MARC field for Content type is 336.

EXAMPLE: 336 text
        336 still image

• Media type—picture books and graphic novels are print items and therefore "unmediated." Non-print items such as models and games are also typically "unmediated." Because audiovisual items require different devices for viewing or accessing information, they are either listed as "audio" or "video" depending on their format. The RDA Summary Sheet will assist with identifying the appropriate media types. The MARC field for Media type is 337.

EXAMPLE: 337 unmediated

• Carrier type—picture books and graphic novels are listed as "volume." All audiovisual items that are not streamed via the Internet are formatted on some kind of material and therefore listed as "audio disc," "videodisc," or "computer disc" depending on their format. The carrier type for most non-print items is "object." The RDA Summary Sheet will assist with identifying the appropriate carrier types. The MARC field for Carrier type is 338.

EXAMPLE: 338   videodisc

STEP 2: Identify information displayed on the item to be transcribed:

- Title—RDA standards require title information to be transcribed from the preferred source of information. Different libraries have different rules regarding capitalization of titles. Title information may be transcribed as represented on the preferred source of information; use local rules or follow a style guide such as the *Chicago Manual of Style*. Use ISBD punctuation to transcribe the title information into the Title and Statement of Responsibility area of the 245 MARC record field.

- Statement of responsibility—RDA standards require statement of responsibility information to be transcribed from the preferred source of information. Audiovisual media often have many creators listed on the preferred source of information. RDA standards state that all creators should be listed in the Statement of Responsibility, but this also can be shortened if necessary. Use ISBD punctuation to transcribe the statement of responsibility information into the Title and Statement of Responsibility area of the 245 MARC record field. The RDA Summary Sheet will assist with format and punctuation.

  EXAMPLE: 245   Hippity Hop Frog Checkers / by Hasbrothers, Inc.

- Creators—RDA standards require creator information be included in the catalog record as a core element. Use the Library of Congress Name Authorities to locate authorized headings, which may include birth and death dates. RDA standards prescribe specific relationship designators to be used. The relationship designators associated with audiovisual and non-print materials vary and include terms such as "narrator," "producer," "actor," "director," and "performer." Picture books and graphic novels will typically have an author and an illustrator. The RDA Summary Sheet will assist with identifying the appropriate relationship designators for each creator. List the author in the 100 MARC field and the illustrator in the 700 MARC field. Audiovisual and non-print items often have no individual author, so typically there is no 100 MARC field entry, except in the cases of audiobooks and performed music CDs. When there is no main author, all the creators are typically listed as contributors in the 700 or 710 fields.

  EXAMPLE: 100   Houston, James, 1951-, author.
  EXAMPLE: 710   Hasbrothers, production company.

- Contributors—RDA standards state that contributors and their relationships such as "actor" or "director" be included in a catalog record. Use the Library of Congress Name Authorities to locate authorized headings, which may include birth and death dates. The RDA Summary Sheet will assist with identifying the appropriate relationship designators. Contributors other than the main author or performer are added to the record in the 700 MARC field if the contributor is a person, or the 710 field if it is a corporate entity.

EXAMPLE: 700   Houston, James, 1951-, narrator.

- Publication information—RDA standards state that information about the publication, manufacture, distribution, or copyright of an item be included in the catalog record, as well as the location and date of this event. Print materials include this information on the title or verso page. Audiovisual and non-print materials typically have production companies and copyright information on the preferred source of information. Use ISBD punctuation to list the name and location of the production company and publication date. If there is a copyright date but no publication date, place the date in brackets and add a field for the copyright date using the copyright symbol. Transcribe the publication location from the preferred source of information. Transcribe the name of the production company from the preferred source of information. Use the copyright symbol if the date is a copyright date. This information is listed in the 264 MARC field.

EXAMPLE: 264   Norwich, Conn. : Hasbrothers, Inc. 2015.

- Edition information—edition information is not often a part of a picture book, graphic novel, or audiovisual resource, but sometimes part of realia, such as board games. If there is an edition statement, transcribe the information from the source of information into the 250 MARC field.

EXAMPLE: 250   Golden Anniversary Edition.

- Series title—both print and audiovisual resources are sometimes part of a series and have a series title listed on the preferred source of information. Transcribe this information into the 490 MARC field and in the 8XX MARC field. In this example, the Uniform Title of the Series is entered into the 830 field.

EXAMPLE: 490   Have fun will travel series, vol. 13
EXAMPLE: 830   Have fun will travel series.

- Identifier for manifestation—picture books and graphic novels generally have ISBN numbers. This information is entered into the 020 MARC field. Standard numbers associated with audiovisual materials such as sound recordings, video recordings, printed music, and other music-related material are called publisher numbers and are found on the preferred source of information. This information is entered into the 028 MARC field. There are often no standardized numbers listed for non-print materials so this information when available is entered into the 024 MARC field. An example of a common standard number for these types of materials is the Universal Product Code 12 digit bar code number.

EXAMPLE: 020   9782349843451

STEP 3: Identify information to be recorded.

- Extent—RDA standards state that the extent of the item, along with its illustrative content and dimensions, be included in the record. In the 300 MARC field, record this information using ISBD punctuation and terminology. Examine the item's contents and preferred source of information. Use the RDA terminology such as "model," "kit," "videodisc," and "audio disc" for media formats. The RDA Summary Sheet will assist with identifying the correct terminology. Do not abbreviate any words except for the length of an audiovisual program, which is measured in hours and minutes. In the area reserved for illustrative content, list information such as the number of pieces if the item is a game, analog or stereo sound, digital video, or color illustrations. The dimension of an item refers to the diameter of the disc, the size of the tape, or length of the container, and is measured in inches.

EXAMPLE: 300   1 audio disc : digital: 4 ¾ in.

- Notes—notes, although not an RDA required core element, do provide essential information about an item and are useful to users as they search the library catalog for information. Typical notes that are part of catalog records include general notes located in the 500 MARC field, formatted contents notes located in the 505 MARC field, summary notes located in the 520 MARC field, system notes in the 538 MARC field, target audience notes in the 521 MARC field, study program notes in the 526 MARC field, and language notes located in the 546 MARC field. Formatted content notes can be used in music CDs to list song titles, composers, featured performers, and timings. System notes are used with audiovisual materials to denote details about requirements for accessing information in digital or analog form.

EXAMPLE: 538   System requirements: Blu-ray DVD player.

STEP 4: Apply subject headings and call numbers.
- Subject headings—Use the *Sears Subject Headings* list to identify the main heading for the item, along with other appropriate headings and subdivisions. Add local subject headings to facilitate searching. Use the 650 MARC field for topical subject headings and the 651 MARC field for geographic headings.

EXAMPLE: 650   Stories in rhyme.

- Call number—picture books and graphic novels, because they are considered to be in some way different from traditional fiction and nonfiction materials, are often shelved in a separate location. This is also the case for audiovisual and non-print materials. Use the local library call number notation system for these materials. If the item is related to a Dewey class, it is often helpful to assign a Dewey number so that these items will appear in the results list of items in that topic area. Here is an example of how a call number for *The Very Hungry Caterpillar* by Eric Carle might be listed:

EXAMPLE: E Carle 2000

STEP 5: Add the item to the catalog and review the entry.

INTERNET RESOURCES

Resource Description and Access Toolkit: http://access.rdatoolkit.org/
Official website for subscription-based RDA Standards resource

Library of Congress Name Authorities: http://authorities.loc.gov/
Authorized name headings

MARC Standards: http://www.loc.gov/marc/
MARC 21 Standards from the Library of Congress

Bibliographic Formats and Standards: http://www.oclc.org/bibformats/en.html
OCLC Standards for MARC records

Classify: An experimental classification web service: http://classify.oclc.org/classify2/
Find Dewey classifications by titles, ISBN numbers, or subjects

Dewey Cutter Program: https://www.oclc.org/support/services/dewey/program.en.html
A software program for PC systems that create Cutter numbers for library items

EXERCISES

Example 1
Audiobook Item Practice Exercise

Marion Librarian: Runaway Scooter Mystery

Joan James with
Dilbert Slathers
audio narration by John James

Marion Librarian audio mystery series number 2
Limited Libraries Audio Collections
New York - copyright 2015

Notes: This audio book is on a CD, is 120 minutes long, and 12 centimeters. The author was born in 1975; the narrator was born in 1975. The series is for children grades 8-12. Publisher number is: CT04291

Summary: Marion Librarian steals a motor scooter to solve the mystery of the disappearing books.

MARC Tag	RDA Element	Field Entry
	Mode of issuance	m
	Local call number	AV James 2015
028	Identifying Number	CT 04291
100	Creator, Relationship Designator	James, Joan, 1975-, author.
245	Title Proper, Other Title Information, Statement of Responsibility	Marion Librarian : Runaway Scooter Mystery / Joan James with Dilbert Slathers ; audio narration by John James.
264	Place of Publication, Publisher's Name, Publication Date	New York : Limited Libraries Audio Collections, [2015]
264	Copyright Date	©2015
300	Extent, Illustrations, Dimensions	1 audio disc (120 min.) : digital ; 12 cm
336	Content Type	spoken word
337	Media Type	audio
338	Carrier Type	audio disc
490	Series Statement	Marion Librarian audio mystery series ; number 2
520	Summary Note	Marion Librarian steals a motor scooter to solve the mystery of the disappearing books.
521	Target Audience Note	Grades 8–12.
650	Sears Topical Heading	Librarians—Fiction.
700	Name added entry	Slathers, Dilbert, author.
700	Name added entry	James, John, narrator.
830	Series Added Entry Uniform Title	Marion Librarian audio mystery series ; number 2

Example 2
Audio CD Item Practice Exercise

COFFEE! Chaos in the Morning
Lana Languish

Coffee

Los Angeles - Independent Music International
copyright 2015

Notes: This 12 centimeter digital audio CD is 60 minutes long;
the author was born in 1975
Publisher number: LL182000

Summary: In her inimitable style Blues singer Lana Languuish
sings about her morning cup of Joe. Songs include Blue Mountain
blend -- On my last nerve -- Cruisin' for a bruisin' -- Ventura Freeway
Starbucks Blues -- Steaming Paradise Cove sunrise -- Coffee cake.

MARC Tag	RDA Element	Field Entry
	Mode of issuance	m
	Local call number	AV Languish 2015
028	Identifying Number	LL182000
100	Creator, Relationship Designator	Languish, Lana, 1975-, performer.
245	Title Proper, Other Title Information, Statement of Responsibility	COFFEE! : Chaos in the Morning / Lana Languish.
264	Place of Publication, Publisher's Name, Publication Date	Los Angeles: Independent Music International, [2015]
264	Copyright Date	©2015
300	Extent, Illustrations, Dimensions	1 audio disc (60 min.) : digital ; 12 cm
336	Content Type	performed music
337	Media Type	audio
338	Carrier Type	audio disc
505	Formatted Contents Note	Blue Mountain blend—On my last nerve—Cruisin' for a bruisin'—Ventura Freeway Starbucks Blues—Steaming Paradise Cove sunrise—Coffee cake.
520	Summary Note	In her inimitable style, Blues singer Lana Languish sings about her morning cup of Joe.
650	Sears Topical Heading	Blues music—United States.

110

Example 3
Audiovisual Item Practice Exercise

Turtle Time Productions presents Turtle Time!

Starring Tommy Turtle and the Turtle Time Band

© 2015
Turtle Time
Productions
Hampton Beach
New York

Notes: This 12 centimeter DVD is a musical animation that is 25 minutes long and contains subtitles in Spanish, English, and French. The item requires a DVD player. This resource is for students from Kindergarten to third grade. Standard Number 5602-7831

Summary: In this animated film, Tommy Turtle returns to his home beach to find true love and reunite the Turtle Time Band.

MARC Tag	RDA Element	Field Entry
	Mode of issuance	m
	Local call number	AV Turtle Time 2015
028	Identifying Number	5602–7831
245	Title Proper, Other Title Information, Statement of Responsibility	Turtle Time Productions presents Turtle Time! / Starring Tommy Turtle and the Turtle Time Band.
264	Place of Publication, Publisher's Name, Publication Date	Hampton Beach, New York : Turtle Time Productions, [2015]
264	Copyright Date	©2015
300	Extent, Illustrations, Dimensions	1 videodisc (25 min.) : sound, color ; 12 cm
336	Content Type	two-dimensional moving image
336	Content Type	performed music
337	Media Type	video
338	Carrier Type	videodisc
520	Summary Note	In this animated film, Tommy Turtle returns to his home beach to find true love and reunite the Turtle Time Band.
521	Target Audience Note	Kindergarten to third grade students.
538	Systems details note	System requirements: DVD player.
546	Language of Content	English. Contains subtitles in Spanish, English, and French.
650	Sears Topical Heading	Turtles—Animated films.
710	Corporate Name Entry	Turtle Time Productions, production company.

Example 4
Print Item Practice Exercise

We are going to the country!
Vamos al campo!

by Lily Magnolia
Spanish translation by Rosa Blanca
illustrations by Diego Rivers

Both Borders Press ©2014
San Diego California

Notes: This 16 x 27 cm bilingual children's picture book has 15 pages, colored illustrations, and maps; the author was born in 1990. The illustrator was born in 1986. This item is for Kindergarten to third grade.
ISBN 972-4-54693-457-5

Summary: The Madera family is taking a trip to the country to visit their cousins who live on a farm.

MARC Tag	RDA Element	Field Entry
	Mode of issuance	m
	Local call number	FIC Magnolia 2014
020	Identifying Number	9724546934575
100	Creator, Relationship Designator	Magnolia, Lily, 1990-, author.
245	Title Proper, Other Title Information, Statement of Responsibility	We are going to the country! Vamos al campo! / by Lily Magnolia ; Spanish translation by Rosa Blanca ; illustrations by Diego Rivers.
264	Place of Publication, Publisher's Name, Publication Date	San Diego, California : Both Borders Press, [2014]
264	Copyright Date	©2014
300	Extent, Illustrations, Dimensions	15 pages : color illustrations, maps ; 27 cm
336	Content Type	text
336	Content Type	still image
337	Media Type	unmediated
338	Carrier Type	volume
520	Summary Note	The Madera family is taking a trip to the country to visit their cousins who live on a farm.
521	Target Audience Note	Kindergarten to third grade.
546	Language of Content	In English and Spanish.
650	Sears Topical Heading	Farm life—Fiction. Bilingual books—English-Spanish.
700	Name added entry	Blanca, Rosa, translator.
700	Name added entry	Rivers, Diego, 1986-, illustrator.

Example 5
Print Item Practice Exercise

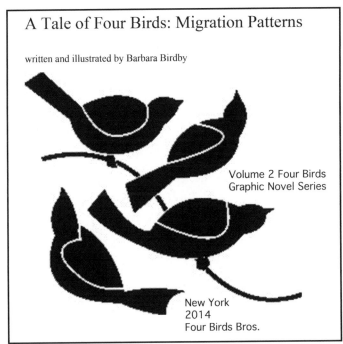

A Tale of Four Birds: Migration Patterns

written and illustrated by Barbara Birdby

Volume 2 Four Birds
Graphic Novel Series

New York
2014
Four Birds Bros.

Notes: This 15 x 22 cm graphic novel has 100 pages, color
illustrations; the author was born in 1980. This item is for
first to fourth grade students.
ISBN 975-3-65813-462-1

Summary: The four birds join forces during migration
season to fend off would be predators.

MARC Tag	RDA Element	Field Entry
	Mode of issuance	m
	Local call number	FIC Birdby 2014
020	Identifying Number	9753658134621
100/110	Creator, Relationship Designator	Birdby, Barbara, 1980-, author, illustrator.
245	Title Proper, Other Title Information, Statement of Responsibility	A Tale of Four Birds : Migration Patterns / written and illustrated by Barbara Birdby.
264	Place of Publication, Publisher's Name, Publication Date	New York : Four Birds Bros., 2014.
300	Extent, Illustrations, Dimensions	100 pages : color illustrations ; 22 cm
336	Content Type	text
336	Content Type	still image
337	Media Type	unmediated
338	Carrier Type	volume
490	Series Statement	Four Birds Graphic Novel Series ; Volume 2
520	Summary Note	The four birds join forces during migration season to fend off would be predators.
521	Target Audience Notes	First to fourth grade.
650	Sears Topical Heading	Birds—Migration—Fiction. Birds—Migration—Graphic novel.
830	Series Added Entry Uniform Title	Four Birds Graphic Novel Series ; Volume 2

Example 6
Realia Item Practice Exercise

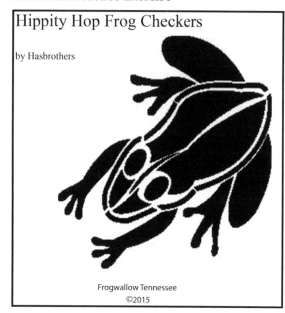

Hippity Hop Frog Checkers

by Hasbrothers

Frogwallow Tennessee
©2015

Notes: This 7 x 40 x 27 cm board game contains 1 game board, 30 question cards, 1 die, 25 checker pieces, 1 instruction sheet. Standard Number 7143-7893

Summary: A game for all ages, this checkers-based board game helps families learn about the species of frogs inhabiting U.S. waterways.

MARC Tag	RDA Element	Field Entry
	Mode of issuance	
	Local call number	
024	Identifying Number	
245	Title Proper, Other Title Information, Statement of Responsibility	
264	Place of Publication, Publisher's Name, Publication Date	
264	Copyright Date	
300	Extent, Illustrations, Dimensions	
336	Content Type	
336	Content Type	
336	Content Type	
337	Media Type	
338	Carrier Type	
520	Summary Note	
521	Target audience note	
650	Sears Topical Heading	
710	Corporate name added entry	

Example 7
Realia Item Practice Exercise

Tenticles! A game of cooperation, chance, and slime
another tantalizing adventure from Octopod Games Inc.

©2014 Octopod Games, Inc.
Calimari Cove California

Note: This 8 x 25 x 27 cm board game has 400 question cards, game board, die, 5 game pieces, and 1 insruction sheet.
Standard Number 7340-2356

Summary: Teams of 2 to 4 players ages 12 to adult vie to be the first to build their giant squid, sink the treasure ship and collect the gold.

MARC Tag	RDA Element	Field Entry
	Mode of issuance	
	Local call number	
024	Identifying Number	
245	Title Proper, Other Title Information, Statement of Responsibility	
264	Place of Publication, Publisher's Name, Publication Date	
264	Copyright Date	
300	Extent, Illustrations, Dimensions	
336	Content Type	
336	Content Type	
336	Content Type	
336	Media Type	
338	Carrier Type	
520	Summary Note	
521	Target audience note	
650	Sears Topical Heading	
690	Local Subject Heading	
710	Creator, Relationship Designator	

Example 8
Audiovisual Item Practice Exercise

Notes: This 4 3/4 inch video DVD is 126 minutes long; is in English, French or Spanish
Standard Number 20153452

Summary: Ben Jones stars as a teenager who turns into a zombie from watching too much television. His girlfriend notices and tries to save him.

MARC Tag	RDA Element	Field Entry
	Mode of issuance	
	Local call number	
028	Identifying Number	
245	Title Proper, Other Title Information, Statement of Responsibility	
264	Place of Publication, Publisher's Name, Publication Date	
264	Copyright Date	
300	Extent, Illustrations, Dimensions	
336	Content Type	
337	Media Type	
338	Carrier Type	
520	Summary Note	
546	Language of Content	
538	Systems details note	
650	Sears Topical Heading	
700	Name added entry	
700	Name added entry	
700	Name added entry	
710	Corporate Name Added Entry	

Example 9
Print Item Practice Exercise

The Black Cat's Return
by Cats Malone

illustrations by Tabby Calico

Graphic Cats Press - Calico Corners California - ©2014

Notes: This 21x 26 cm graphic novel has 125 pages, color illustrations;the author was born in 1959. ISBN 971-2-47707-210-5

Summary: Cats Malone entertains us with the misadventures of his cat "Blackie" in this graphic novel.

MARC Tag	RDA Element	Field Entry
	Mode of issuance	
	Local call number	
020	Identifying Number	
100	Creator, Relationship Designator	
245	Title Proper, Other Title Information, Statement of Responsibility	
264	Place of Publication, Publisher's Name, Publication Date	
264	Copyright Date	
300	Extent, Illustrations, Dimensions	
336	Content Type	
336	Content Type	
337	Media Type	
338	Carrier Type	
520	Summary Note	
650	Sears Topical Heading	
700	Name added entry	

Example 10
Print Item Practice Exercise

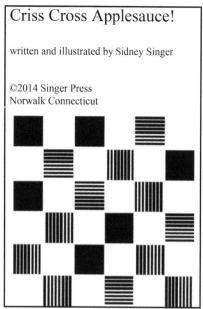

Criss Cross Applesauce!

written and illustrated by Sidney Singer

©2014 Singer Press
Norwalk Connecticut

This 7 x 9 cm board book has 20 pages and color illustrations. ISBN 981-2-78323-468-9; the author was born in 1976.

Summary: The author uses colorful illustations and engaging rhymes to guide young children in to sit quietly in a cross-legged position for storytime activities.

MARC Tag	RDA Element	Field Entry
	Mode of issuance	
	Local call number	
020	Identifying Number	
100	Creator, Relationship Designator	
245	Title Proper, Other Title Information, Statement of Responsibility	
264	Place of Publication, Publisher's Name, Publication Date	
264	Copyright Date	
300	Extent, Illustrations, Dimensions	
336	Content Type	
336	Content Type	
337	Media Type	
338	Carrier Type	
520	Summary Note	
650	Sears Topical Heading	

9

Cataloging Electronic Resources

INTRODUCTION

The electronic resources collection in the school library comprises a variety of materials such as selected websites, blogs, and multimedia online resources. These materials are widely used by teachers and students in every curricular area and in every grade level. Maintaining and updating this virtual collection of resources is an essential function of a 21st-century library. Because new items are added to the web continuously, making sure that electronic resources are cataloged and integrated into the library OPAC is a big task for school librarians who are already inundated with work. For this reason, developing skills in cataloging electronic resources and developing an efficient workflow process are essential for meeting the challenges of the 21st-century school library.

CATALOGING ELECTRONIC MATERIALS

Before beginning cataloging electronic resources, it is important to consider the items in their relation to the physical library collection, particularly how they might add to or enhance the existing collection. In this way, the cataloging process will be connected to the overall mission of the library and help users locate and access information. Electronic resources that are typically added to the school library catalog include those that support the school curriculum such as websites and blogs. Other items might include resources that meet the extracurricular interests of users in the areas of sports, hobbies, and popular culture. The workflow for cataloging these items follows the process discussed in previous chapters with specific instructions for electronic materials. The remainder of this chapter contains five completed catalog records and five practice catalog records with answers located in the Appendix. To gain practice in cataloging these materials, examine the completed records and use them as a model to complete the five remaining records.

WORKFLOW FOR ELECTRONIC RESOURCES

STEP 1: Identify what is being cataloged and enter information about the following:

- Preferred source of information—RDA standards have designated the title or "home" page of electronic resources to be the preferred source of information. Additional information is typically located in the "about" or "contact us" pages of a website. Most of the information required for completing catalog records for these items will be found on the preferred source of information.

- Mode of issuance—mode of issuance for most website materials will be "integrating resource" because they are updated continuously. The MARC notation in the LDR/07 area of the record is the letter **i** for integrating resource. This information is generally entered into the catalog record automatically when a specific type of item is selected for cataloging using the ILS cataloging module.

  EXAMPLE: LDR/07   i

- Content type—Internet resources have a number of possible content types and therefore may contain multiple entries in this field such as "text," "still image," "spoken word," "performed music," and "video." The MARC field for Content type is 336.

  EXAMPLE: 336   text
            336   performed music
            336   video

- Media type—because websites and blogs require a mediating device for viewing or accessing information, they are listed as "computer." The MARC field for Media type is 337.

  EXAMPLE: 337   computer

- Carrier type—online resources are all virtual items, and therefore the carrier type is listed as "online resource." The MARC field for Carrier type is 338.

  EXAMPLE: 338   online resource

STEP 2: Identify information displayed on the item to be transcribed:

- Title—RDA standards state that title information is to be transcribed from the preferred source of information. Libraries have different rules for capitalizing title information. Some libraries transcribe the title information as represented on the item, while other libraries have their own rules or use a style guide such as the *Chicago Manual of Style*. Use ISBD punctuation to transcribe the title information into the Title and Statement of Responsibility area of the 245 MARC record field.
- Statement of responsibility—RDA standards state that the Statement of Responsibility information is to be transcribed from the preferred source of information. RDA standards state that all contributors listed on the item be included in the Statement of Responsibility, but libraries have some flexibility about following this rule. Use ISBD punctuation to transcribe the Statement of Responsibility information into the Title and Statement of Responsibility area of the 245 MARC record field.

EXAMPLE: 245   Media3693 Studios : Mixed Media Art Quilts / by Cindy Houston.

- Creators—RDA standards state that creator information is to be included in the record as a core element. Use the Library of Congress Name Authority headings to locate authorized headings, which may include birth and death dates. The relationship designator associated with electronic resources, in which there is an identifiable creator, is typically "author." The 100 MARC record field is used for individual authors; the 110 MARC field is used for a corporate name. Often websites have no identifiable creator, so this tag is left blank and contributors are listed in the MARC 700 or 710 fields.

EXAMPLE: 100   Houston, Cynthia, 1959-, author.
EXAMPLE: 710   Modern Association of School Librarians, issuing body.

- Contributors—RDA standards state that contributors and their relationships such as "narrator" or "performer" be included in a catalog record. Use the Library of Congress Name Authorities to locate authorized headings, which may include birth and death dates. Contributors other than the main author are added to the record in the 700 MARC field if the contributor is a person, or the MARC 710 field if it is a corporate entity. Organizations associated with websites are typically referred in the relationship designator as the "issuing body."

EXAMPLE: 710   Wildlife Society, issuing body.

- Publication information—RDA rules require that information about the publication, manufacture, distribution, or copyright of an item be included in the catalog record, as well as the location and date of this event. Electronic materials typically have publisher and copyright information listed on the bottom of the title screen or in the "about" or "contact us" areas of the website. Use ISBD punctuation to list the location of the publisher, manufacturer or distributor, and the name of the company. If a publication date is not listed but a copyright date is listed, put the date in brackets and list the copyright date with copyright symbol in a separate field entry. Transcribe the publication location and the website publisher name from the preferred source of information. If the location of the website publisher is known but not listed on the website, surround the publication location with brackets. This information is listed in the 264 MARC field.

EXAMPLE: 264   [New York] : Media3693Studios, [2015]
         264   ©2015.

- Edition information—edition information is rarely listed for electronic resources because they are continuously updated. If edition information is listed on the website, transcribe this information into the 250 MARC field.

EXAMPLE: 250   Special Edition.

- Series title—electronic resources rarely include series information. If this information is listed on the website, transcribe it from the preferred source of information into the 490 MARC tag and as an added entry in the 800s MARC field.

EXAMPLE: 490   Et tu Barbae? Mystery Series ; vol. 7
EXAMPLE: 830   Et tu Barbae? Mystery Series.

- Identifier for manifestation—standard numbers are rarely associated with electronic materials. If they do exist, transcribe this information into the 024 MARC Record field. A website will always have an Internet address, and this information is entered into the "Electronic location and access" 856 MARC field.

EXAMPLE: 024   PL4598
          856   http://www.media3693studios.com

STEP 3: Identify information to be recorded.

- Extent—RDA standards state that the extent of the item, along with its illustrative content and dimensions, be included in the record. Record this information in the 300 MARC field using ISBD punctuation from an examination of the item's home page and navigational links. Record the item as an online resource. Use the term "illustrations" if there are only black-and-white illustrations and "color illustrations" if they are in color. Additional media types that may be included in the illustrative content are listed in the Appendix. Electronic resources have no dimensions.

EXAMPLE: 300   1 online resource : digital, sound, color illustrations.
EXAMPLE: 300   1 online resource (44 pages) : color illustrations.

- Notes—notes, although not an RDA core element, do provide essential information about an item and help users search the library catalog for information. Typical notes that are part of catalog records for electronic resources include general notes, located in the 500 MARC field, summary notes located in the 520 MARC field, target audience notes located in the 521 field, study program notes located in the 526 field, and language notes located in the 546 field. When cataloging websites, it is customary to note the viewing date in the 500 field of the MARC record. Typically, the navigational links of electronic resources, which supply information about the contents of the site, are listed in the formatted contents notes located in the 505 MARC field.

EXAMPLE: 500   Viewed on March 1, 2016.
EXAMPLE: 505   Artist Statement—Gallery—See My Work!—ETSY!

- Electronic location and access—all websites have an associated URL designating their location on the Internet. Include the URL of the title page of the item in the 856 MARC field of the MARC record.

STEP 4: Apply Subject Headings, Classification, and Call Numbers.

- Subject headings—use the *Sears Subject Headings* list to identify the main heading for the item, along with other appropriate headings and subdivisions. Add local subject headings to facilitate searching.

EXAMPLE: 650   Women artists—Internet resources.

- Classification—although electronic items do not have call numbers because they are not located on library shelves, adding a Dewey classification to the catalog record will enable users to find websites and other electronic resources when conducting a search by Dewey classification.
- Call number—electronic items do not have call numbers, but it is useful to add them to the catalog by listing the Dewey classification so they will be included in the results of searching activities using Dewey numbers.

EXAMPLE: 709.2

STEP 5: Add the item to the catalog and review the entry.

INTERNET RESOURCES

Resource Description and Access Toolkit: http://access.rdatoolkit.org/
Official website for subscription-based RDA Standards resource

Library of Congress Name Authorities: http://authorities.loc.gov/
Authorized name headings

MARC Standards: http://www.loc.gov/marc/
MARC 21 Standards from the Library of Congress

Bibliographic Formats and Standards: http://www.oclc.org/bibformats/en.html
OCLC Standards for MARC records

Classify: An experimental classification web service: http://classify.oclc.org/classify2/
Find Dewey classifications by titles, ISBN numbers, or subjects

Dewey Cutter Program: https://www.oclc.org/support/services/dewey/program.en.html
A software program for PC systems that create Cutter numbers for library items

EXERCISES

Example 1
Electronic Item Practice Exercise

URL://www.wildchess.com

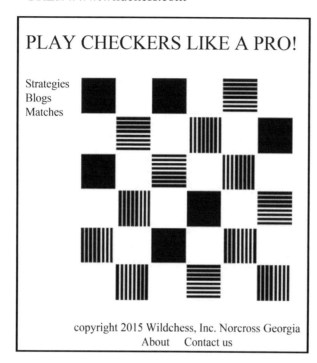

PLAY CHECKERS LIKE A PRO!

Strategies
Blogs
Matches

This website has color diagrams, streaming video, and podcasts.

Summary: Website for beginning checkers players who want to win more matches.

copyright 2015 Wildchess, Inc. Norcross Georgia
About   Contact us

MARC Tag	RDA Element	Field Entry
	Mode of issuance	i
	Local call number	794.2
245	Title Proper, Other Title Information, Statement of Responsibility	PLAY CHECKERS LIKE A PRO! / Wildchess, Inc.
264	Place of Publication, Publisher's Name, Publication Date	Norcross, Georgia : Wildchess, Inc., [2015]
264	Copyright Date	©2015.
300	Extent, Illustrations, Dimensions	1 online resource : digital, sound, color illustrations.
336	Content Type	text
336	Content Type	still image
336	Content Type	spoken word
336	Content Type	two-dimensional moving image
337	Media Type	computer
338	Carrier Type	online resource
505	Formatted contents notes	Strategies—Blogs—Matches.
520	Summary Note	Website for beginning checkers players who want to learn strategy and win more matches.
650	Sears Topical Heading	Checkers—Strategic aspects.
710	Corporate Name added entry	Wildchess, Inc., issuing body.
856	Electronic location and access	http://www.wildchess.com

Example 2
Electronic Item Practice Exercise

URL:http://www.wls.org/frogchronicles

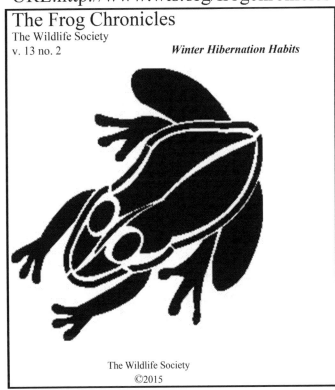

The Frog Chronicles
The Wildlife Society
v. 13 no. 2   *Winter Hibernation Habits*

The Wildlife Society
©2015

Notes: This ezine features 40 pages and color photos
ISSN 7173-7871

Summary: The Wildlife Society publication for upper
elementary students focusing specifically on frog
habitats and behavior. Published in Washington, D.C.
but this is not listed on the ezine.

MARC Tag	RDA Element	Field Entry
	Mode of issuance	i
	Local call number	597.8
022	Identifying Number	7173–7871
245	Title Proper, Other Title Information, Statement of Responsibility	The Frog Chronicles / The Wildlife Society.
264	Place of Publication, Publisher's Name,	[Washington, D.C.] : The Wildlife Society, [2015]
264	Copyright Date	©2015.
300	Extent, Illustrations, Dimensions	1 online resource (40 pages) : color illustrations.
336	Content Type	text
336	Media Type	still image
337	Media Type	computer
338	Carrier Type	online resource
520	Summary Note	The Wildlife Society ezine publication for upper elementary students focusing specifically on frog habitats and behavior.
521	Target audience note	Elementary grades
650	Sears Topical Heading	Frogs–Behavior.
710	Corporate Name Added Entry	Wildlife Society, issuing body.
856	Electronic Location and access	http://www.wls.org/frogchronicles

Example 3
Electronic Item Practice Exercise

URL: http://www.coffee_encylopedia.org

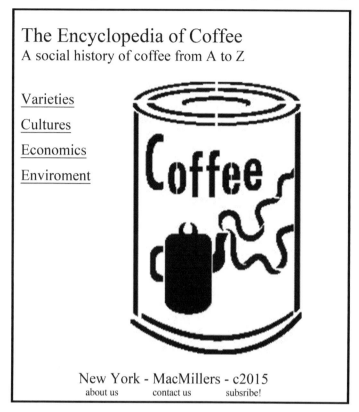

The Encyclopedia of Coffee
A social history of coffee from A to Z

Varieties

Cultures

Economics

Enviroment

Notes: This continuously updated website features color photographs and maps

Summary: This is a subscription based website featuring the social, cultural and economic history of coffee

New York - MacMillers - c2015

about us   contact us   subsribe!

MARC Tag	RDA Element	Field Entry
	Mode of issuance	i
	Local call number	641.8
245	Title Proper, Other Title Information, Statement of Responsibility	The Encyclopedia of Coffee : A social history of coffee from A to Z / MacMillers.
264	Place of Publication, Publisher's Name,	New York : MacMillers, [2015]
264	Copyright Date	©2015.
300	Extent, Illustrations, Dimensions	1 online resource : color illustrations, maps.
336	Content Type	text
336	Content Type	still image
337	Media Type	computer
338	Carrier Type	online resource
505	Formatted contents note	Varieties—Cultures—Economics—Environment.
520	Summary Note	This is a subscription-based website featuring the social, cultural, and economic history of coffee.
650	Sears Topical Heading	Coffee—Social aspects. Coffee—Encyclopedia.
710	Corporate Name added entry	MacMillers, issuing body.
856	Electronic location and access	http://www.coffee_encylopedia.org

Example 4
Electronic Item Practice Exercise

URL: http://www.wls.org/SOS

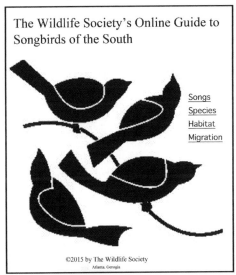

The Wildlife Society's Online Guide to Songbirds of the South

Songs
Species
Habitat
Migration

©2015 by The Wildlife Society
Atlanta, Gerogia

Notes: This online guidebook contains 300 pages of color photographs and audio files of birdsongs.

Summary: A comprehensive online pictoria guide to the south's species of songbirds and audio recordings of their birdsongs.

MARC Tag	RDA Element	Field Entry
	Mode of issuance	i
	Local call number	598
245	Title Proper, Other Title Information, Statement of Responsibility	The Wildlife Society's Online Guide to Songbirds of the South / The Wildlife Society.
264	Place of Publication, Publisher's Name,	Atlanta, Georgia : The Wildlife Society, [2015]
264	Copyright Date	©2015.
300	Extent, Illustrations, Dimensions	1 online resource (300 pages) : digital, sound, color illustrations.
336	Content Type	text
336	Content Type	still image
336	Content Type	sounds
337	Media Type	computer
338	Carrier Type	online resource
505	Formatted contents notes	Songs—Species—Habitat—Migration.
520	Summary Note	A comprehensive online pictorial guide to the South's species of songbirds and audio recordings of their birdsongs.
650	Sears Topical Heading	Birds—United States. Birds—Southern states. Birdsongs.
710	Corporate Name Added Entry	Wildlife Society, issuing body.
856	Electronic location and access	http://www.wls.org/SOS

Example 5
Electronic Item Practice Exercise

URL:http://www.michelindamin.com/OETT

Michelindamin's Online Encyclopedia of Travel andTourism

North America
South America
Europe
Asia

Michelindamin, Inc. ©2014
New York - Paris

Notes: This continuously updated online encyclopedia contains 450 pages of description and color photographs.

Summary: Michelindamin's covers the world with an encyclopedia devoted to the independent world traveler. This reference tool contains travel information by geographic region.

MARC Tag	RDA Element	Field Entry
	Mode of issuance	i
	Local call number	910
245	Title Proper, Other Title Information, Statement of Responsibility	Michelindamin's Online Encyclopedia of Travel and Tourism / Michelindamin, Inc.
264	Place of Publication, Publisher's Name, Publication Date	New York ; Paris ; Michelindamin, Inc., [2014]
264	Copyright Date	©2014.
300	Extent, Illustrations, Dimensions	1 online resource (450 pages) : color illustrations.
336	Content Type	text
336	Content Type	still image
337	Media Type	computer
338	Carrier Type	online resource
505	Formatted Contents Notes	North America—South America—Europe—Asia.
520	Summary Note	Michelindamin covers the world with an encyclopedia devoted to the independent world traveler. This reference tool contains travel information by geographic region.
650	Sears Topical Heading	Travel—Encyclopedia.
710	Corporate Author Added Entry	Michelindamin, Inc., issuing body.
856	Electronic location and access	http://www.michelindamin.com/OETT

Example 6
Electronic Item Practice Exercise

URL: http://www.wordpress.com/weeklyworst

The Weekly Worst
Television's worst weekly shows

written by Daniel Pinkney and Sharon Stubbins

This Week

Archive

2013 Best of the Worst

2012 Best of the Worst

2011 Best of the Worst

copyright 2015 - 21st Century Worstfest - Los Angeles
contact us!

Notes: This weekly blog has color photos, audio and video clips

Summary: Bloggers Daniel Pinkney and Sharon Stubbins share their opinions on the best and worst weekly television shows.

MARC Tag	RDA Element	Field Entry
	Mode of issuance	
	Local call number	
100	Creator, Relationship Designator	
245	Title Proper, Other Title Information, Statement of Responsibility	
264	Place of Publication, Publisher's Name, Publication Date	
264	Copyright Date	
300	Extent, Illustrations, Dimensions	
336	Content Type	
336	Content Type	
336	Content Type	
336	Content Type	
337	Media Type	
338	Carrier Type	
505	Formatted contents notes	
520	Summary Note	
650	Sears Topical Heading	
700	Name added entry	
856	Electronic location and access	

Example 7
Electronic Item Practice Exercise

URL:http://www.dailyoctopus.nanu.edu

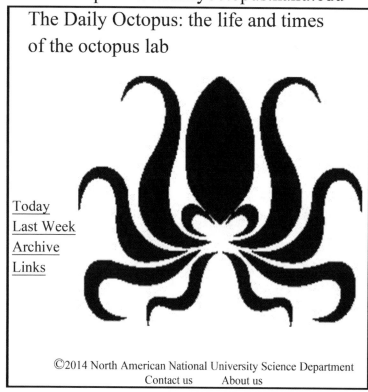

The Daily Octopus: the life and times of the octopus lab

Today
Last Week
Archive
Links

Note: Published in Bar Harbor, Maine, but this information is not listed. This blog contains color photos and narrated videos.

Summary: The octopus lab at NANU is a hive of activity. View the latest observations of octopus behavior and learn about new discoveries from the scientists in this daily blog.

©2014 North American National University Science Department
Contact us   About us

MARC Tag	RDA Element	Field Entry
	Mode of issuance	
	Local call number	
245	Title Proper, Other Title Information, Statement of Responsibility	
264	Place of Publication, Publisher's Name, Publication Date	
264	Copyright Date	
300	Extent, Illustrations, Dimensions	
336	Content Type	
336	Content Type	
336	Content Type	
336	Content Type	
337	Media Type	
338	Carrier Type	
505	Formatted Contents Notes	
520	Summary Note	
650	Sears Topical Heading	
690	Local Subject Heading	
710	Corporate Name added entry	
856	Electronic location and access	

Example 8
Electronic Item Practice Exercise

URL: http://www.turtlewatchers.org

Turtle Watchers International

WEST   EAST

Weekly Watch
Write!
Donate!

© 2015 Turtle Watchers International
Hampton Beach, New York

Contact Us   About the Site

Notes: This website has color photographs, streaming audio and video. It is updated weekly.

Summary: Oganizational website for Turtle Watchers International a group monitoring
turle migrations on the east and west coasts of the United States.

MARC Tag	RDA Element	Field Entry
	Mode of issuance	
	Local call number	
245	Title Proper, Other Title Information, Statement of Responsibility	
264	Place of Publication, Publisher's Name, Publication Date	
264	Copyright Date	
300	Extent, Illustrations, Dimensions	
336	Content Type	
336	Content Type	
336	Content Type	
336	Content Type	
337	Media Type	
338	Carrier Type	
505	Formatted Contents Note	
520	Summary Note	
650	Sears Topical Heading	
710	Corporate Name Added Entry	
856	Electronic location and access	

Example 9
Electronic Item Practice Exercise

URL http://blackcatrecipebarn.com

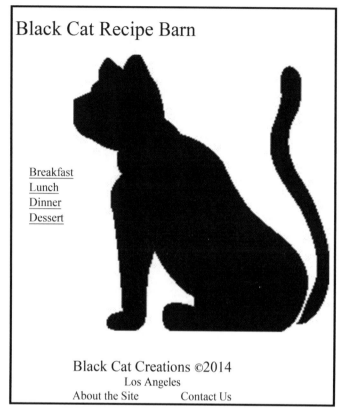

Notes: This website contains color photographs of food and preparation procedures.

Summary: Companion website to the famous Los Angeles restaurant, the Black Cat, it features recepies for favorite restaurant dishes.

MARC Tag	RDA Element	Field Entry
	Mode of issuance	
	Local call number	
245	Title Proper, Other Title Information, Statement of Responsibility	
264	Place of Publication, Publisher's Name, Publication Date	
264	Copyright Date	
300	Extent, Illustrations, Dimensions	
336	Content Type	
336	Content Type	
337	Media Type	
338	Carrier Type	
505	Formatted contents note	
520	Summary Note	
650	Sears Topical Heading	
650	Sears Topical Heading	
710	Name added entry	

Example 10
Electronic Item Practice Exercise

URL: http://www.masl.org/msl

The Modern School Librarian
by the Modern Association of School
Librarians (MASL) Chicago, Illinois
volume 12 issue 7
©2014

The mobile librarian issue

Notes: This ezine contains 70 pages of articles,
color photos, and videos
ISSN 0317-8471

Summary: MSL features innovative librarians and
programming ideas throughout the United States.

MARC Tag	RDA Element	Field Entry
	Mode of issuance	
	Local call number	
022	Identifying Number	
245	Title Proper, Other Title Information, Statement of Responsibility	
264	Place of Publication, Publisher's Name, Publication Date	
264	Copyright Date	
300	Extent, Illustrations, Dimensions	
336	Content Type	
336	Content Type	
336	Content Type	
336	Content Type	
337	Media Type	
338	Carrier Type	
490	Series Added Entry	
520	Summary Note	
650	Sears Topical Heading	
710	Corporate Name Added Entry	
830	Series Added Entry Uniform Title	
856	Electronic location and access	

10

Cataloging Electronic Streaming Resources

INTRODUCTION

Adding virtual resources such as streaming video and audio to the library catalog enhances the library collection without a great deal of added cost. Curating a collection of quality streaming programs in digital format is an essential function of a 21st-century school library. Because it is possible to add digital resources to the collection continuously, making sure that they are included in the online catalog quickly and correctly does pose a challenge, but the added labor pays off handsomely in terms of the quality resources that these items contribute to the collection.

CATALOGING ELECTRONIC STREAMING MATERIALS

Before beginning to catalog electronic streaming resources, think about how these digital items can enhance the library collection, how they can be integrated into the library catalog, and how users might search for information by subject and format. This will help streamline the workflow process and help users locate and access information. Electronic streaming audio and video resources that are added to the school library catalog may include adaptations of literature that support the school literacy program, or nonfiction programs in the social, physical, and life sciences that support the school curriculum. Other materials might include streaming programming that meets the interests of the school population in the area of sports or popular culture. The workflow for cataloging these items is similar to other materials with specific rules for streaming electronic resources and is outlined in the following text. The remainder of the chapter contains five completed catalog records and five practice catalog records with answers located in the Appendix. To gain practice in cataloging these materials, examine the completed records and use them as a model to complete the five remaining records. Use the RDA Summary Sheet in the Appendix of this book to help with applying RDA standards and ISBD punctuation to specific areas of the MARC record.

WORKFLOW FOR ELECTRONIC STREAMING RESOURCES

STEP 1: Identify what is being cataloged and enter information about the following:

- Preferred source of information—RDA standards state that the title screen of video and audio streaming resources and the title or home page of websites are the preferred sources of information. Additional information is typically located in the "about" or "contact us" sections of the resource. Most of the information required for completing catalog records for streaming items will be found on these sources of information.

- Mode of issuance—mode of issuance for most streaming video programs will be a single unit for both video and audio streaming programs. In both cases, the MARC notation on the LDR/07 area of the record is the letter **m** for monograph. This information is typically added automatically to the record when a cataloger selects the type of resource in the ILS cataloging module.

EXAMPLE: LDR/07   m

- Content type—audio and video streaming materials may contain a variety of content types including "spoken word" for audio podcasts, "two-dimensional moving image" for streaming video or vodcasts, and possibly "performed music," "still image," and even "text." The MARC field for Content type is 336.

EXAMPLE: 336   spoken word
          336   performed music

- Media type—because streaming media are accessed on the Internet, the media type is "computer." The MARC field for Media type is 337.

EXAMPLE: 337   computer

- Carrier type—streaming media are located on the Internet, and therefore the carrier type is "online resource." The MARC field for Carrier type is 338.

EXAMPLE: 338   online resource

STEP 2: Identify information displayed on the item to be transcribed:

- Title—RDA standards state that title information is to be transcribed from the preferred source of information. Libraries use different rules for capitalization in this area. Some libraries transcribe the information from the item, while others follow their own rules or use a style guide such as the *Chicago Manual of Style*. Use ISBD punctuation to transcribe the title information into the Title and Statement of Responsibility area of the 245 MARC record field.
- Statement of responsibility—RDA standards specify that Statement of Responsibility information be transcribed from the preferred source of information. RDA states that all of the responsible creators listed should be included in the record, but libraries also have some flexibility about how many to include. Use ISBD punctuation to transcribe the statement of responsibility information into the Title and Statement of Responsibility area of the 245 MARC record field.

EXAMPLE: 245   The Frog Chronicles : Podcast 15 / produced by the Wildlife Society.

- Creators—RDA standards state that creator information be included in the record as a core element. Use the Library of Congress Name Authorities to locate authorized headings, which may include birth and death dates. Some video and audio podcasts do not have a single creator, and therefore there is no 100 tag for many of these entries.

EXAMPLE: 100   Stubbins, Mark, 1975-, performer, narrator.

- Contributors—RDA standards state that contributors and their relationships such as "producer" or "narrator" be included in a catalog record. Use the Library of Congress Name Authorities to locate authorized headings, which may include birth and death dates. In most video and audio productions, there are many contributors. These personal names are entered into the 700 field. Corporate names are entered into the 710 field.

EXAMPLE: 710   Wildlife Society Video Productions, production company.

- Publication information—RDA standards state that information about the production, distribution, and publication date of an item be included in the catalog record, as well as the location and date of this event. Streaming materials typically have production and copyright information listed in the preferred source of information. Use ISBD punctuation to list the name and location of the production company and publication date. If there is no publication date listed, but a copyright date is listed, place the date in brackets and add an additional entry for the copyright date. Transcribe the publisher name and location as listed on the item. This information is listed in the 264 MARC field.

EXAMPLE: 264   London : International Productions, Inc., [2015]
         264   ©2015.

- Edition information—edition information is not typically an element of a streaming resource. If there is edition information, transcribe it from the preferred source of information into the 250 MARC field.

EXAMPLE: 250   Golden Anniversary Edition.

- Series title—streaming resources that are part of a series will often have a series title listed on the preferred source of information. Transcribe this into the 490 MARC tag, and as an added entry, list the formal title of the series in the 800s MARC field.

EXAMPLE: 490   The Mobile Librarian Video Series ; number 5
EXAMPLE: 830   Mobile Librarian Video Series.

- Identifier for manifestation—streaming audio and video resources do not typically have standard numbers. If there is a number associated with the item, it can be listed in the 024 Other Standard Number MARC field.

EXAMPLE: 024   7693–2

STEP 3: Identify information to be recorded:

- Extent—RDA states that the extent of the item, along with its illustrative contents, be included in the record. Streaming media do not have a dimension, so this subfield is omitted. Record the extent in the 300 MARC field using ISBD punctuation. Streaming media are listed as an "online resource" with the file type, length of the program recorded in hours and minutes, and any other illustrative content. Do not abbreviate any words except for the length of the program.

EXAMPLE: 300   1 online resource (1 video file (20 min.)) : digital, sound, color.
EXAMPLE: 300   1 online resource (1 audio file (45 min.)) : digital, sound.

- Notes—notes, although not an RDA core element, do provide essential information about an item and are useful to users as they search the library catalog for information. Typical notes that are part of catalog records for streaming resources include general notes, located in the 500 MARC field, formatted contents notes located in the 505 MARC field, summary notes located in the 520 MARC field, target audience notes located in the 521 MARC field, study program notes located in the 526 MARC field, and language notes located in the 546 MARC field. Electronic streaming resources often will include a viewing date listed in the 500 MARC field.

EXAMPLE: 500   Viewed on March 15, 2016.
EXAMPLE: 546   English, with Spanish subtitles.

- Electronic location and access—the 856 field is an important MARC tag for Internet resources. In this field, list the complete URL for accessing the streaming resource.

EXAMPLE: 856   http://www.youtoob.com/wildlifepodcasts/

STEP 4: Apply subject headings, classification, and call numbers.

- Subject Headings—use the *Sears* Subject Headings list to identify the main heading for the item, along with other appropriate headings and subdivisions. Add local subject headings to facilitate searching.

EXAMPLE: 650   Television programs—Reviews.

- Classification—although electronic streaming resources do not require a call number, it is useful to assign a Dewey classification number so that users can find these resources when browsing by Dewey number.
- Call number—because streaming media do not occupy a space on the library shelf, no additional notation is needed other than the Dewey classification, which is useful for students when they are browsing for information by Dewey class.

EXAMPLE: 756.3

STEP 5: Add the item to the catalog and review the entry.

INTERNET RESOURCES

Resource Description and Access Toolkit: http://access.rdatoolkit.org/
Official website for subscription-based RDA Standards resource

Library of Congress Name Authorities: http://authorities.loc.gov/
Authorized name headings

MARC Standards: http://www.loc.gov/marc/
MARC 21 Standards from the Library of Congress

Bibliographic Formats and Standards: http://www.oclc.org/bibformats/en.html
OCLC Standards for MARC records

Classify: An experimental classification web service: http://classify.oclc.org/classify2/
Find Dewey classifications by titles, ISBN numbers, or subjects

Dewey Cutter Program: https://www.oclc.org/support/services/dewey/program.en.html
A software program for PC systems that create Cutter numbers for library items

EXERCISES

Example 1
Streaming Item Practice Exercise

URL: http://www.wordpress.com/weeklyworst/episode1

The Weekly Worst
Television's worst weekly shows
Episode 1

written and narrated by Daniel Pinkney and Sharon Stubbins

This Week

Archive

2013 Best of the Worst
2012 Best of the Worst
2011 Best of the Worst

Notes: This weekly series is a vodcast 20 minutes long in color. Pinkney was born in 1986. Stubbins was born in 1992.

Summary: Vodcasters Daniel Pinkney and Sharon Stubbins share their opinions on the best and worst weekly television shows.

The Weekly Worst Series

copyright 2015 - 21st Century Worstfest - Los Angeles
contact us!

MARC Tag	RDA Element	Field Entry
	Mode of issuance	m
	Local call number	791.45
100	Creator, Relationship Designator	Pinkney, Daniel, 1986-, author, narrator.
245	Title Proper, Other Title Information, Statement of Responsibility	The Weekly Worst : Television's worst weekly shows Episode 1 / written and narrated by Daniel Pinkney and Sharon Stubbins.
264	Place of Publication, Publisher's Name, Publication Date	Los Angeles : 21st Century Worstfest [2015]
264	Copyright Date	©2015.
300	Extent, Illustrations, Dimensions	1 online resource (1 video file (20 min.)) : digital, sound, color.
336	Content Type	two-dimensional moving image
336	Content Type	spoken word
337	Media Type	computer
338	Carrier Type	online resource
490	Series Statement	The Weekly Worst Series ; Episode 1
520	Summary Note	Vodcasters Daniel Pinkney and Sharon Stubbins share their opinions on the best and worst weekly television shows.
650	Sears Topical Heading	Television programs—Reviews.
700	Name added entry	Stubbins, Sharon, 1992-, author, narrator.
830	Series Added Entry Uniform Title	The Weekly Worst Series ; Episode 1.
856	Electronic location and access	http://www.wordpress.com/weeklyworst/episode1

Example 2
Streaming Item Practice Exercise

URL: http://www.coffeecast.com/greenmountain

Coffecast 21
Green Mountain Coffee

Varieties

Cultures

Economics

Enviroment

Coffeecast Series #21
Los Angeles - New York
MacMillers Productions - c2013
about us   contact us   subscribe!

Notes: This 30 minute video program features color
video, audio narration and musical performances

Summary: This is a streaming video program
featring the community life surrounding
the Green Mountain Coffee Plantation.

MARC Tag	RDA Element	Field Entry
	Mode of issuance	m
	Local call number	641.8
245	Title Proper, Other Title Information, Statement of Responsibility	Coffeecast 21 : Green Mountain Coffee / MacMillers Productions.
264	Place of Publication, Publisher's Name, Publication Date	Los Angeles ; New York : MacMillers Productions, [2013]
264	Copyright Date	©2013.
300	Extent, Illustrations, Dimensions	1 online resource (1 video file (30 min.)) : digital, sound, color.
336	Content Type	two-dimensional moving image
336	Content Type	spoken word
336	Content Type	performed music
337	Media Type	computer
338	Carrier Type	online resource
490	Series Statement	Coffeecast Series ; #21
520	Summary Note	This is a streaming video program featuring the community life surrounding the Green Mountain Coffee Plantation.
650	Sears Topical Heading	Coffee—Social aspects.
830	Series Added Entry Uniform Title	Coffeecast Series ; #21.
856	Electronic location and access	http://www.coffeecast.cm/greenmountain

Example 3
Streaming Item Practice Exercise
URL:http://www.dailyoctopus.nanu.edu/ollie

The Daily Octopus: the life and times of Ollie the Octopus Week 5

Today
Last Wee
Archive
Links

Note: This 15 minute streaming video contains clips of Ollie the Octopus and audio narration. The vodcast is produced in Bar Harbor, Maine but is not listed on the web site.

Summary: The octopus lab at NANU is a hive of activity. This week Ollie the Octopus rearranges the furniture.

©2014 North American National University Science Department

Contact us   About us

MARC Tag	RDA Element	Field Entry
	Mode of issuance	m
	Local call number	591.77
245	Title Proper, Other Title Information, Statement of Responsibility	The Daily Octopus : the life and times of Ollie the Octopus Week 5 / North American National University Science Department.
264	Place of Publication, Publisher's Name, Publication Date	[Bar Harbor, Me.] : North American National University Science Department, [2014]
264	Copyright Date	©2014.
300	Extent, Illustrations, Dimensions	1 online resource (1 video file (15 min.)) : digital, sound, color.
336	Content Type	two-dimensional moving image
336	Content Type	spoken word
337	Media Type	computer
338	Carrier Type	online resource
520	Summary Note	The octopus lab at NANU is a hive of activity. This week Ollie the Octopus rearranges the furniture.
650	Sears Topical Heading	Marine animals—Study and teaching.
690	Local Subject Heading	Octopus—Behavior.
710	Corporate Name added entry	North American National University Science Department, issuing body.
856	Electronic location and access	http://www.dailyoctopus.nanu.edu/ollie

Example 4
Streaming Item Practice Exercise

URL:http://www.masl.org/msl/podcast15

The Modern School Librarian Podcast
no. 15: Bookmobile Dos and Don'ts
produced by the Modern Association of School
Librarians
copyright 20

Modern School Librarian Podcast Series no. 15

Notes: This 30 minute podcast contains audio narration
and performed music. This podcast is produced in Chicago
but this information is not listed on the site. The narrator
was born in 1975.

Summary: MASL podcast 15 features tips for bookmobile
librarians by librarian Rocky Bullwinkle on temperature
management and crowd control, and includes a performance
of "Don't Rock my Boat" by the by the Tired Librarians.

MARC Tag	RDA Element	Field Entry
	Mode of issuance	m
	Local call number	025.5
245	Title Proper, Other Title Information, Statement of Responsibility	The Modern School Librarian Podcast no. 15 : Bookmobile Dos and Don'ts / produced by the Modern Association of School Librarians.
264	Place of Publication, Publisher's Name,	[Chicago, Ill.] : Modern Association of School Librarians, [2014]
264	Copyright Date	©2014.
300	Extent, Illustrations, Dimensions	1 online resource (1 audio file (30 min.)) : digital, sound.
336	Content Type	spoken word
336	Content Type	performed music
337	Media Type	computer
338	Carrier Type	online resource
490	Series Statement	The Modern School Librarian Podcast ; no. 15.
520	Summary Note	MASL podcast 15 features tips for bookmobile librarians by librarian Rocky Bullwinkle on temperature management and crowd control, and includes a performance of "Don't Rock my Boat" by the Tired Librarians.
650	Sears Topical Heading	Library services. School libraries—Associations.
700	Name added entry	Bullwinkle, Rocky, 1975-, narrator.
710	Corporate name added entry	Tired Librarians, performers.
710	Corporate name added entry	Modern Association of School Librarians, production company.
830	Series Added Entry Uniform Title	Modern School Library Podcast ; no. 15.
856	Electronic location and access	http://www.masl.org/msl/podcast15

Example 5
Streaming Item Practice Exercise

URL http://blackcatrecipebarn.com/breadpudding

Black Cat Recipe Barn Episode 5:
Kitty's Bread Pudding

Breakfast
Lunch
Dinner
Dessert

Black Cat Recipe Barn Series no. 5
produced by Black Cat Creations ©2014
Los Angeles
About the Site   Contact Us

Notes: This 30 minute streaming video shows preparation procedures. Kitty Katter was born in 1959.

Summary: Kitty Katter, owner of the famous Los Angeles restaurant, the Black Cat, demonstrates how to prepare her favorite bread pudding dessert.

MARC Tag	RDA Element	Field Entry
	Mode of issuance	m
	Local call number	641.86
245	Title Proper, Other Title Information, Statement of Responsibility	Black Cat Recipe Barn Episode 5 : Kitty's Bread Pudding / produced by Black Cat Creations.
264	Place of Publication, Publisher's Name, Publication Date	Los Angeles : Black Cat Creations, [2014]
264	Copyright Date	©2014.
300	Extent, Illustrations, Dimensions	1 online resource (1 video file (30 min.)) : sound, color.
336	Content Type	two-dimensional moving image
336	Content Type	spoken word
337	Media Type	computer
338	Carrier Type	online resource
490	Series statement	Black Cat Recipe Barn Series ; no. 5
520	Summary Note	Kitty Katter, owner of the famous Los Angeles restaurant, the Black Cat, demonstrates how to prepare her favorite bread pudding dessert.
650	Sears Topical Heading	Desserts. Cooking. Restaurants—California.
710	Corporate Name added entry RDA 20.2, 18.5; Appendix I.3.1	The Black Cat, production company.
700	Name added entry RDA 20.2, 18.5; Appendix I.3.1	Katter, Kitty, 1959-, actor.
830	Series Added Entry Uniform Title	Black Cat Recipe Barn Series ; no. 5.
856	Electronic location and access	http://blackcatrecipebarn.com/breadpudding

Example 6
Streaming Item Practice Exercise

URL: http://www.wls.org/SOSreport

The Wildlife Society Presents: Songbirds of
the South Migration Update produced by the
Wildlife Society Songbird Productions

Songs
Species
Habitat
Migration

Atlanta, Georgia ©2015

Notes: This 30 minute online video news report
contains video clips, color photographs and
audio narration

Summary: Weekly migration update covers the
south's species of songbirds migration to Florida.

MARC Tag	RDA Element	Field Entry
	Mode of issuance	
	Local call number	
245	Title Proper, Other Title Information, Statement of Responsibility	
264	Place of Publication, Publisher's Name, Publication Date	
264	Copyright Date	
300	Extent, Illustrations, Dimensions	
336	Content Type	
336	Content Type	
336	Content Type	
337	Media Type	
338	Carrier Type	
520	Summary Note	
650	Sears Topical Heading	
710	Corporate Name added entry	
856	Electronic location and access	

Example 7
Streaming Item Practice Exercise

URL:http://www.michelindaminmotoring.com/alps

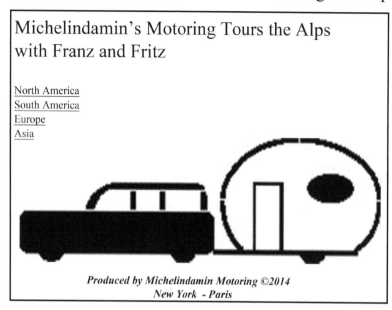

Michelindamin's Motoring Tours the Alps
with Franz and Fritz

North America
South America
Europe
Asia

Produced by Michelindamin Motoring ©2014
New York - Paris

Notes: This streaming video program is 30 minutes long with narration and video clips. Hosts Fritz and Franz Frankenthaler were born in 1980.

Summary: Michelindamin's Motoring tours the Swiss Alps with local tour guides Franz and Fritz Frankenthaler. The program highlights the sights and sounds of the region and reviews the best spots for motor camping.

MARC Tag	RDA Element	Field Entry
	Mode of issuance	
	Local call number	
245	Title Proper, Other Title Information, Statement of Responsibility	
250	Edition Statement	
264	Place of Publication, Publisher's Name, Publication Date	
264	Copyright Date	
300	Extent, Illustrations, Dimensions	
336	Content Type	
336	Content Type	
337	Media Type	
338	Carrier Type	
520	Summary Note	
651	Sears Geographic Heading	
700	Name Added Entry	
700	Name Added Entry	
710	Corporate Name Added Entry	
856	Electronic location and access	

Example 8
Streaming Item Practice Exercise

URL: http://www.turtlewarchers.org/GeorgeLanders

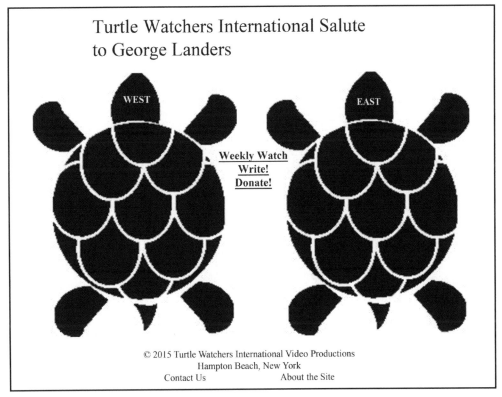

Turtle Watchers International Salute
to George Landers

WEST   EAST

Weekly Watch
Write!
Donate!

© 2015 Turtle Watchers International Video Productions
Hampton Beach, New York
Contact Us   About the Site

Notes: This 60 minute streaming video has audio narration, video clips,
performed music, and color photographs

Summary: Video production features biography of George Landers (1945-2014), famous
turtle scientist and founding father of Turtle Watchers International . The program includes video
clips, narration by scientist Leonard Nimrod, historical color photographs, and a musical
performance by the Turtle Time band.

MARC Tag	RDA Element	Field Entry
	Mode of issuance	
	Local call number	
245	Title Proper, Other Title Information, Statement of Responsibility	
264	Place of Publication, Publisher's Name, Publication Date	
264	Copyright Date	
300	Extent, Illustrations, Dimensions	
336	Content Type	
336	Content Type	
336	Content Type	
336	Content Type	
337	Media Type	
338	Carrier Type	
520	Summary Note	
650	Sears Topical Heading	
600	Name Subject Heading	
700	Personal Name Added Entry	
710	Corporate Name Added Entry	
710	Corporate Name Added Entry	
856	Electronic location and access	

Example 9
Streaming Item Practice Exercise

URL:http://www.wls.org/frogchronicles/Pondpod15

The Frog Chronicles Podcast 15
produced by The Wildlife Society
Podcast number 15

The Wildlife Society Audio Productions
©2015

Notes: This 12 minute podcast features audio narration. The podcast is produced in Washington, D.C. but this is not listed on the site.

Summary: The Wildlife Society weekly podcast for upper elementary students focusing specifically on frog habitats and behavior.

MARC Tag	RDA Element	Field Entry
	Mode of issuance	
	Local call number	
245	Title Proper, Other Title Information, Statement of Responsibility	
264	Place of Publication, Publisher's Name, Publication Date	
264	Copyright Date	
300	Extent, Illustrations, Dimensions	
336	Content Type	
337	Media Type	
338	Carrier Type	
490	Series Statement	
520	Summary Note	
521	Target audience note	
650	Sears Topical Heading	
710	Corporate Name added entry	
830	Series Uniform Title	
856	Electronic location and access	

Example 10
Streaming Item Practice Exercise

URL://www.wildchess.com/wildopeners

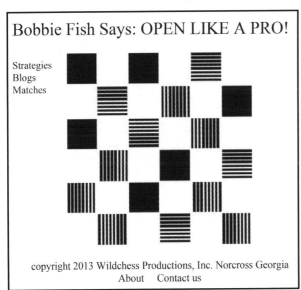

Bobbie Fish Says: OPEN LIKE A PRO!

Strategies
Blogs
Matches

copyright 2013 Wildchess Productions, Inc. Norcross Georgia
About   Contact us

This 20 minute vodcast has color diagrams, and audio narration. Narrator Robert Fish was born in 1972.

Summary: Chess master Bobbie Fish narrates this program on winning with wild and aggressive opening moves.

MARC Tag	RDA Element	Field Entry
	Mode of issuance	
	Local call number	
245	Title Proper, Other Title Information, Statement of Responsibility	
264	Place of Publication, Publisher's Name, Publication Date	
264	Copyright Date	
300	Extent, Illustrations, Dimensions	
336	Content Type	
336	Content Type	
337	Media Type	
338	Carrier Type	
520	Summary Note	
650	Sears Topical Heading	
700	Name added entry	
710	Corporate Name added entry	
856	Electronic location and access	

Appendix

Appendix Table 1.1
MARC and RDA Summary Sheet

MARC Tag/RDA Core Element	RDA Rule	Rule	Example
Identifier for the Manifestation: LCCN 010 ISBN 020 ISSN 022 Other Standard Identifier 024 Publisher 028	CH 2 CH 2 CH 2	Choose an internationally recognized identifier; transcribe it as listed in source of information, omit hyphens. Take LCCN number from Library of Congress record. Take ISBN number from preferred source of information, eliminate dashes. Take ISSN number from preferred source of information, eliminate dashes. If no other number is available, the Universal Product Code (Barcode) is a useful standard identifier	LCCN 8401–8492 ISBN 9789070002343 ISSN 0046225X Publisher number VU098
Local call Number:		This is developed by the cataloger using LC or DDC classification, work marks, dates, and Cutter numbers, and no RDA rules apply; virtual items such as websites should use Dewey Classification only	Nonfiction title 027.4 Potter 2009 fiction title FIC Grant 2005 biography title B Woods 2009 website 302
Heading Personal Name 100 Heading Corporate Name 110	CH 9 AP A AP D AP M	Choose the name author is commonly known and list in the following order: last name, first name, birth date, and death date. Capitalize first word and proper names. End entry with a full stop or period. For variant names of Corporate Names, add Tracing note (tag 410). Use Library of Congress Authorities to find Personal Name Heading and Corporate Names	Smith, John, 1832–1911, author. United Nations Council on Aging, issuing body.
Title and Statement of Responsibility: 245	CH 2 AP A AP D AP M	Title and SOR are transcribed from the preferred source of information such as the book or CD title page, meaning you key it in as it is written! Transcribe the title as it appears on the preferred source of information (title page, cover, etc.). Precede the subtitle with a colon. Precede the first statement of responsibility with a diagonal slash. Precede each subsequent statement of responsibility with a semicolon. End entry with a full stop or period	The Little Prince : The story of a boy / Antoine de Saint-Exupéry ; Richard Howard. Duck feathers : The Story of Silliness / by John Smith, Jane Doe, Bob Brown.
Variant Title 246	CH 2	Record variant title if important	Alice in Wonderland. Alice's Adventures in Wonderland.
Edition: 250	CH 2 CH 2 AP A	Edition statement is transcribed from the preferred source of information such as the book cover or title page. Brackets may be added if clarification is needed or if information is known but not listed on item. End entry with a full stop or period	Second edition. 2nd [edition] Abridged / by Ruth Fraser.

Publication information: 264 CH 2 AP D AP B	Publisher's name and place of publication information is transcribed from the preferred source of information; if there is more than one publisher or location place, only one is required but if used, place them in order listed on information source; publication place should include city and larger jurisdiction. If publication location, publisher, or date are known but not listed, add in brackets.	Westport, Conn : Libraries Unlimited, 1998. [New York] : Scribner, [2010] New York ; London; Victoria (AU) : Haworth Press, Inc., [2005] ©2005.
	Precede the publisher information by a colon, the publication or copyright date by a comma Use abbreviations for states from abbreviations list (see below) Add the copyright symbol only if the source of information states that the date is a copyright date; otherwise, it's a publication date and does not use copyright symbol. For items with a copyright date, place the date in brackets and add another entry for the copyright date. Use the copyright symbol. End entry with a full stop or period	
Series Statement: 490 CH 2 AP A	Transcribe the title of the series from the title page or other source of information Add Series Added Entry tag (830) Volume numbers, etc., are transcribed from the preferred source of information no full stop needed	Discovering America Series ; Vol. 1, no. 1 830 Discovering America Series. Volume 1, no. 1
Mode of Issuance:	single unit, serial, multipart monograph, integrating resource Book, Video, Audio Song (single unit) Magazine (serial) Encyclopedia (multipart monograph) Website (integrating resource) no full stop needed	single unit "m" serial "s" multipart monograph "m" integrating resource "i"
Extent or Physical Description: 300 CH 3 CH 7 AP D	Record the number of units, appropriate carrier, illustrative contents, dimensions Precede other technical details (i.e., other than extent or dimensions) by a colon. Precede dimensions by a semicolon. Precede each statement of accompanying material by a plus sign. For non-book items, use the materials designator appropriate for the item (see later) no full stop needed Selected materials types: pages, audio disk, videodisk, online resource, game	3 audio discs (3 hrs.) : digital; 4 ¾ in. 1 computer disc : digital, sound ; 12 cm + insert. xxvii, 417 pages ; 26 cm 286 pages : illustrations ; 22 cm 1 online resource (1 video file (26 min.)) : digital, sound, color.

(Continued)

Appendix Table 1.1 (*Continued*)

MARC Tag/RDA Core Element	RDA Rule	Rule	Example
		Selected file types: audio file, data file, image file, program file, text file, video file Selected illustrative content terms: illustrations, color illustrations, maps, digital, sound, color	
Content Type: 336		List all the content types appropriate to item: text, spoken word, performed music, moving image cartographic dataset cartographic image, cartographic moving image, cartographic tactile image, cartographic tactile three-dimensional form, cartographic three-dimensional form computer dataset, computer program, notated movement, notated music, performed music, sounds, spoken word, still image, tactile image, tactile music, tactile notated movement, tactile text, tactile three-dimensional form, text, three-dimensional form, three-dimensional moving image, two-dimensional moving image no full stop needed	two-dimensional moving image spoken word performed music text still image
Media Type: 337	CH 3	List media type from the following: audio, computer, microform, microscopic, projected, stereographic, unmediated (books are unmediated), video no full stop needed	video
Carrier Type: 338	CH 3	List carrier type; see complete list at the end of this document AUDIO: audio cartridge, audio disc, audiocassette, audiotape reel COMPUTER: computer disc, computer disc cartridge, online resource UNMEDIATED: card, flipchart, roll, sheet, volume (a book is a volume) VIDEO: video cartridge, videocassette, videotape reel no full stop needed	online resource

154

Field	Description	Code	Examples
Notes: General 500 Bibliography 504 Formatted Contents 505 Summary Notes 520 Target Audience 521 Study Program 526 System Details 538 Language Note 546	General Note: Take information for a note from any source; note source of title information if taken from source other than title page; Make a note of the date an online resource was viewed Bibliography Note: note if item contains a bibliography and/or index Formatted Contents note: denote chapters or song titles separated by— Summary notes: summary description of item Target Audience notes: note if item is targeted or limited to specific age or grade level Study Program notes: Describe reading program information such as AR or school wide big read System Details notes: Descriptive information important for being able to access information such as computer system or "mode of access" Language Note: Language(s) of content	CH 2	500 Title taken from container. 500 Title from cover. 500 Viewed Jan. 13, 2016. 504 Includes bibliographic references. 504 Includes bibliographic references and index. 504 Includes index. 505 How these records were discovered—A short sketch of the Talmuds—Constantine's letter. 520 This site has information about J.R.R. Tolkien, the books he wrote, his life, books others have written about him, the Society and its events. 521 Young Adult. 526 Accelerated Reader AR. 538 System requirements: IBM PC AT or XT; CD-ROM player and drive. 538 Mode of Access: World Wide Web. 546 In English with Spanish and French Subtitles
Topical Subject Heading: 650	Determined by the cataloger and approved subject heading list		Frogs—Encyclopedia. Frontier and pioneer life—Kentucky.
Personal Name Added Entry 700	Determined by the cataloger and approved authority heading list such as the Library of Congress Name Authorities; Add relationship designator (see later)	AP I	Twain, Mark, 1835–1910, author. Howard, Richard, 1985-, illustrator.
Corporate Name Added Entry 710	Determined by the cataloger and approved authority heading list such as the Library of Congress Name Authorities; Add relationship designator (see the list following)	AP I	Greenpeace International, issuing body. School of Teacher Education. Western Kentucky University, issuing body.
Series Added Entry: 830	List series title from 490 tag		Discovering America Series.
Location Access: 856	List website		http://www.wku.edu

(Continued)

300 TAG Physical Description or Extent-Specific Materials Designations

Print Materials	Electronic Resources	Three-Dimensional Artifacts and Realia	Graphic Materials	Cartographic Materials	Sound Recording	Motion Pictures and Videorecordings
pages	computer card	art original	activity card	atlas	audio cartridge	video cartridge
leaves	computer chip	art reproduction	art original	diagram	audio cassette	videocassette
plates	cartridge	braille cassette	art print	globe	audio cylinder	videotape reel
	computer disc	diorama	art reproduction	map	audio disc	videodisc
	computer disc	exhibit	chart	model	audio roll	
	cartridge	game	filmslip	Profile	audio tape reel	
	computer tape	microscope slide	filmstrip	remote-sensing	sound-track reel	
	cartridge	mock-up	flash card	image section		
	computer tape	model	flip chart	view		
	cassette		photograph			
	computer tape		picture			
	reel		postcard			
	online resource		poster			
	File Types for		radiograph			
	Electronic		slide			
	Resources		stereograph			
	audio file		study print			
	data file		technical drawing			
	image file		transparency			
	program file		wall chart			
	text file					
	video file					

338 TAG RDA Carrier Types

Audio Disc. A disc on which sound waves, recorded as modulations, pulses, etc., are incised or indented in a continuous spiral groove.

Audiocassette. A cassette containing an audio tape.

Audiotape Reel. An open reel holding a length of audio tape to be used with reel-to-reel audio equipment.

Computer Disc. A disc containing digitally encoded data, magnetically or optically recorded.

Online Resource. A digital resource accessed by means of hardware and software connections to a communications network.

Microfiche. A sheet of film bearing a number of microimages in a two-dimensional array.

Microfilm. A film bearing a number of microimages in linear array.

Microopaque. A card or sheet of opaque material bearing a number of microimages in a two-dimensional array.

Film Reel. An open reel holding a motion picture film to be used with a motion picture film projector.

Filmstrip. A roll of film, with or without recorded sound, containing a succession of images intended for projection one at a time.

Overhead Transparency. A sheet of transparent material (with or without a protective mount) bearing an image designed for use with an overhead projector.

Slide. A small sheet of transparent material (usually in a protective mount) bearing an image designed for use with a slide projector or viewer.

Card. A small sheet of opaque material.

Object. A three-dimensional artifact (or a replica of an artifact) or a naturally occurring object.

Sheet. A flat piece of thin material (paper, plastic, etc.).

Volume. One or more sheets bound or fastened together to form a single unit.

Videocassette. A cassette containing a video tape.

Videodisc. A disc on which video signals, with or without sound, are recorded.

Videotape Reel. An open reel holding a video tape for use with reel-to-reel video equipment.

700 & 710 TAG Added Entries: Relationship Designators for Persons and Corporate Bodies

author
compiler
composer
filmmaker
photographer
programmer
director of photography
film director
film producer
issuing body
actor
biographee

narrator
director
publisher
production company
television director
television producer
editor
illustrator
performer
translator
film distributor

157

CHAPTER 6 ANSWERS

Appendix Table 6.5

MARC	RDA Element	Field Entry
	Mode of issuance	m
	Local call number	Fic Carroll 2012
020	Identifying Number	9780141197302
100	Creator, Relationship Designator	Carroll, Lewis, 1832–1898, author.
245	Title Proper, Other Title Information, Statement of Responsibility	Lewis Carroll's Alice's Adventures in Wonderland / with artwork by Yayoi Kusama.
264	Place of Publication, Publisher's Name, Publication Date	London ; New York : Penguin Classics, 2012.
300	Extent, Illustrations, Dimensions	181 pages ; color illustrations ; 23 cm
336	Content Type	text
337	Media Type	still image
337	Media Type	unmediated
338	Carrier Type	volume
650	Sears Topical Heading	Rabbits—fiction.
650	Sears Topical Heading	Fantasy fiction.

CHAPTER 7 ANSWERS

Example 6
Print Item Practice Answers

MARC Tag	RDA Element	Field Entry
	Mode of issuance	m
	Local call number	613.2 Jitters 2015
020	Identifying Number	9413816384571
100	Creator, Relationship Designator	Jitters, Janet, 1975-, author.
245	Title Proper, Other Title Information, Statement of Responsibility	COFFEE! Our Favorite Addiction / by Janet Jitters.
250	Edition Statement	4th edition.
264	Place of Publication, Publisher's Name, Publication Date	Seattle, Washington : Starbucks and Sons publishers, 2015.
300	Extent, Illustrations, Dimensions	200 pages ; 23 cm
336	Content Type	text
337	Media Type	unmediated
338	Carrier Type	volume
490	Series Statement	Common Addictions series ; v. 4
504	Bibliographic/Supplementary Content Note	Includes bibliographical references.
520	Summary Note	Many of us cannot go a day without our morning cup of Joe, but we never consider the health effects of caffeine addiction. This book describes the process by which we become addicted to coffee and the side effects of this habit.
650	Sears Topical Heading	Caffeine—Education. Coffee—Education.
690	Local Topical Heading	Addiction—Education.
830	Series Added Entry—Uniform Title	Common Addictions Series ; v. 4.

Example 7
Print Item Practice Answers

MARC Tag	RDA Element	Field Entry
	Mode of issuance	m
	Local call number	FIC James 2013
020	Identifying Number	9813516384072
100	Creator, Relationship Designator	James, Joan, 1986-, author.
245	Title Proper, Other Title Information, Statement of Responsibility	Runaway Librarian : A Marion Librarian Mystery / Joan James with Dilbert Slathers.
264	Place of Publication, Publisher's Name, Publication Date	New York : Limited Libraries, 2013.
300	Extent, Illustrations, Dimensions	250 pages ; 23 cm
336	Content Type	text
337	Media Type	unmediated
338	Carrier Type	volume
490	Series Statement	Marion Librarian Mystery
520	Summary Note	Join Marion Librarian on her motor scooter mystery tour of the English countryside. This story features a visit to Downtown Abbey, where she solves the murder of Mr. Green Jeans.
650	Sears Topical Heading	Librarians—Mystery fiction.
651	Geographic Heading	England—Mystery fiction.
700	Name added entry	Slathers, Dilbert, author.
830	Series Added Entry—Uniform Title	Marion Librarian Mystery.

Example 8
Print Item Practice Answers

MARC Tag	RDA Element	Field Entry
	Mode of issuance	m
	Local call number	591.77 Calimari 2014
020	Identifying Number	9418517336072
100	Creator, Relationship Designator	Calimari, Oliver, 1972-, author.
245	Title Proper, Other Title Information, Statement of Responsibility	The Kraken Myth : Large Underwater Sea Creatures and their Mythological Origins / Oliver Calimari and Sidney Squidler ; with illustrations by Inkver Fisk.
250	Edition Statement	3rd revised edition.
264	Place of Publication, Publisher's Name, Publication Date	Bangor, Maine : Calimari Bros. Press, 2014.
300	Extent, Illustrations, Dimensions	iv, 250 pages : illustrations ; 26 cm
336	Content Type	Text
336	Content Type	still image
337	Media Type	unmediated
338	Carrier Type	volume
490	Series Statement	The strange and terrifying sea series ; vol. 2

(Continued)

Example 8 *(Continued)*

MARC Tag	RDA Element	Field Entry
504	Bibliographic/Supplementary Content Note	Contains bibliographic references and index.
520	Summary Note	Legends abound about the sea monsters inhabiting our deep oceans. The authors of this book link mythical see monsters such as krakens with large sea life recently discovered on deep ocean dives.
650	Sears Topical Heading	Marine animals—Legends.
700	Name added entry	Squidler, Sidney, author.
700	Name added entry	Fisk, Inkver, illustrator.
830	Series Added Entry Uniform Title	The strange and terrifying sea series ; vol. 2.

Example 9
Print Item Practice Answers

MARC Tag	RDA Element	Field Entry
	Mode of issuance	M
	Local call number	Mag 796.7 NTC 2015
022	Identifying Number	2571–8034
245	Title Proper, Other Title Information, Statement of Responsibility	Life on the Road Magazine : An Insider's Guide to Motor Touring our National Parks / published by National Touring Clubs (NTC).
264	Place of Publication, Publisher's Name, Publication Date	[Las Vegas, Nev.] : National Touring Clubs (NTC), 2015.
300	Extent, Illustrations, Dimensions	250 pages : color illustrations, maps ; 27 cm
336	Content Type	Text
336	Content Type	still image
337	Media Type	unmediated
338	Carrier Type	volume
490	Series Statement	Destination Yellowstone ; January 2015 issue
504	Bibliographic/Supplementary Content Note	Includes bibliographic references.
520	Summary Note	The January 2015 issue focuses on winter touring at Yellowstone National Park.
650	Sears Topical Heading	Travel trailers and campers—Guidebooks. National parks and reserves—United States.
830	Series Added Entry Uniform Title	Destination Yellowstone ; January 2015 issue.

Example 10
Print Item Practice Answers

MARC Tag	RDA Element	Field Entry
	Mode of issuance	m
	Local call number	Mag 794.2 Chess 2015
022	Identifying Number	2771–6534
245	Title Proper, Other Title Information, Statement of Responsibility	Chess Magazine's Chess Secrets for the Wild at Heart / Chess Periodical Press.
264	Place of Publication, Publisher's Name, Publication Date	New York : Chess Periodical Press, 2015.

MARC Tag	RDA Element	Field Entry
300	Extent, Illustrations, Dimensions	50 pages : illustrations ; 9 cm
336	Content Type	text
336	Content Type	still image
337	Media Type	unmediated
338	Carrier Type	volume
490	Series Statement	Chess Secrets Series Special Edition ; CSS volume 17
500	Summary Note	Use chess masters' "Wild at Heart" strategies to win your next timed matches.
650	Sears Topical Heading	Chess—Strategic aspects.
710	Corporate Author Added Entry	Chess Periodical Press, publisher.
830	Series Added Entry—Uniform Title	Chess Secrets Series Special Edition ; volume 17.

CHAPTER 8 ANSWERS

Example 6: Audiovisual Item Practice Answers

MARC Tag	RDA Element	Field Entry
	Mode of issuance	m
	Local call number	Game 597.8 2015
024	Identifying Number	7143–7893
245	Title Proper, Other Title Information, Statement of Responsibility	Hippity Hop Frog Checkers / by Hasbrothers.
264	Place of Publication, Publisher's Name, Publication Date	Frogwallow, Tennessee : Hasbrothers, [2015] ©2015.
264	Copyright Date	
300	Extent, Illustrations, Dimensions	1 game (1 game board, 30 question cards, 1 die, 25 checker pieces, 1 instruction sheet) ; 7 × 40 × 27 cm
336	Content Type	three-dimensional form
336	Content Type	text
336	Content Type	still image
337	Media Type	unmediated
338	Carrier Type	object
520	Summary Note	A game for all ages, this checkers-based board game helps families learn about the species of frogs inhabiting the U.S. waterways.
521	Target audience note	All ages.
650	Sears Topical Heading	Frogs—Board games.
710	Corporate name added entry	Hasbrothers, distributor.

Example 7
Audiovisual Item Practice Answers

MARC Tag	RDA Element	Field Entry
	Mode of issuance	m
	Local call number	Game Tenticles 2014
024	Identifying Number	7340–2356

(Continued)

Example 7 (Continued)

MARC Tag	RDA Element	Field Entry
245	Title Proper, Other Title Information, Statement of Responsibility	Tenticles! A game of cooperation, chance, and slime : another tantalizing adventure / from Octopod Games Inc.
264	Place of Publication, Publisher's Name, Publication Date	Calimari Cove, California : Octopod Games, Inc., [2014] ©2014.
264	Copyright Date	
300	Extent, Illustrations, Dimensions	1 game (400 question cards, game board, die, 5 game pieces, and 1 instruction sheet) ; 8 × 25 × 27 cm
336	Content Type	three-dimensional form
336	Content Type	text
336	Content Type	still image
336	Media Type	unmediated
338	Carrier Type	object
520	Summary Note	Teams of 2–4 players ages 12 to adult vie to be the first to build their giant squid, sink the treasure ship and collect the gold.
521	Target audience note	Ages 12 to adult.
650	Sears Topical Heading	Board games.
690	Local Topical Subject Heading	Cooperative games.
710	Creator, Relationship Designator	Octopod Games, Inc., distributor.

Example 8
Audiovisual Item Practice Answers

MARC Tag	RDA Element	Field Entry
	Mode of issuance	m
	Local call number	AV Teenage Zombie 2015
028	Identifying Number	20153452
245	Title Proper, Other Title Information, Statement of Responsibility	I was a Teenage Zombie / a 21st Century Monsters production ; Starring Ben Jones and Amanda Zong ; written and produced by Rob Zombie.
264	Place of Publication, Publisher's Name, Publication Date	Los Angeles,: 21st Century Monsters Inc., [2015] ©2015.
264	Copyright Date	
300	Extent, Illustrations, Dimensions	1 videodisc (126 min.) : digital, sound, color ; 4 ¾ in.
336	Content Type	two-dimensional moving image
337	Media Type	video
338	Carrier Type	videodisc
520	Summary Note	Ben Jones stars as a teenager who turns into a zombie from watching too much television. His girlfriend notices and tries to save him.
546	Language of Content	English, French, or Spanish.
538	Systems details note	System requirements: DVD player.

MARC Tag	RDA Element	Field Entry
650	Sears Topical Heading	Zombies—Horror films. Teenagers—Horror films.
700	Name added entry	Jones, Ben, actor.
700	Name added entry	Zong, Amanda, actor.
700	Name added entry	Zombie, Rob, writer, producer.
710	Corporate Name Added Entry	21st Century Monsters Inc., production company.

Example 9
Audiovisual Item Practice Answers

MARC Tag	RDA Element	Field Entry
	Mode of issuance	m
	Local call number	FIC Malone 2014
020	Identifying Number	9712477072105
100	Creator, Relationship Designator	Malone, Cats, 1959-, author.
245	Title Proper, Other Title Information, Statement of Responsibility	The Black Cat's Return / by Cats Malone ; illustrations by Tabby Calico.
264	Place of Publication, Publisher's Name, Publication Date	Calico Corners, California : Graphic Cats Press, [2014]
264	Copyright Date	
300	Extent, Illustrations, Dimensions	125 pages : color illustrations ; 26 cm
336	Content Type	text
336	Content Type	still image
337	Media Type	unmediated
338	Carrier Type	volume
520	Summary Note	Cats Malone entertains us with the misadventures of his cat "Blackie" in this graphic novel.
650	Sears Topical Heading	Cats—Fiction. Cats—Graphic novels.
700	Name added entry	Calico, Tabby, illustrator.

Example 10
Audiovisual Item Practice Answers

MARC Tag	RDA Element	Field Entry
	Mode of issuance	m
	Local call number	E Singer 2014
020	Identifying Number	9812783234689
100	Creator, Relationship Designator	Singer, Sidney, 1976-, author, illustrator.
245	Title Proper, Other Title Information, Statement of Responsibility	Criss Cross Applesauce! / written and illustrated by Sidney Singer.
264	Place of Publication, Publisher's Name, Publication Date	Norwalk, Connecticut : Singer Press, [2014]

(Continued)

Example 10(*Continued*)

MARC Tag	RDA Element	Field Entry
264	Copyright Date	©2014
300	Extent, Illustrations, Dimensions	20 pages : color illustrations ; 9 cm
336	Content Type	text
336	Content Type	still image
337	Media Type	unmediated
338	Carrier Type	volume
520	Summary Note	The author uses colorful illustrations and engaging rhymes to guide young children in how to sit quietly in a cross-legged position for story time activities.
650	Sears Topical Heading	Stories in rhyme. Board books for children.

CHAPTER 9 ANSWERS

Example 6
Electronic Item Practice Answers

MARC Tag	RDA Element	Field Entry
	Mode of issuance	i
	Local call number	791.45
100	Creator, Relationship Designator	Pinkney, Daniel, author.
245	Title Proper, Other Title Information, Statement of Responsibility	The Weekly Worst : Television's worst weekly shows / written by Daniel Pinkney and Sharon Stubbins.
264	Place of Publication, Publisher's Name, Publication Date	Los Angeles : 21st Century Worstfest, [2015]
264	Copyright Date	©2015
300	Extent, Illustrations, Dimensions	1 online resource : digital, sound, color illustrations.
336	Content Type	text
336	Content Type	still image
336	Content Type	sounds
336	Content Type	two-dimensional moving image
337	Media Type	computer
338	Carrier Type	online resource
505	Formatted contents notes	This Week—Archive—2013 Best of the Worst—2012 Best of the Worst—2011 Best of the Worst.
520	Summary Note	Bloggers Daniel Pinkney and Sharon Stubbins share their opinions on the best and worst weekly television shows.
650	Sears Topical Heading	Television programs—Reviews.
700	Name added entry	Stubbins, Sharon, author.
856	Electronic location and access	http://www.wordpress.com/weeklyworst

Example 7
Electronic Item Practice Answers

MARC Tag	RDA Element	Field Entry
	Mode of issuance	i
	Local call number	591.77
245	Title Proper, Other Title Information, Statement of Responsibility	The Daily Octopus : the life and times of the octopus lab / North American National University Science Department.
264	Place of Publication, Publisher's Name, Publication Date	[Bar Harbor, Me.] : North American National University Science Department, [2014]
264	Copyright Date	©2014.
300	Extent, Illustrations, Dimensions	1 online resource : digital, sound, color illustrations.
336	Content Type	text
336	Content Type	still image
336	Content Type	sounds
336	Content Type	two-dimensional moving image
337	Media Type	computer
338	Carrier Type	online resource
505	Formatted Contents Notes	Today—Last Week—Archive—Links.
520	Summary Note	The octopus lab at NANU is a hive of activity. View the latest observations of octopus behavior and learn about new discoveries from the scientists in this daily blog.
650	Sears Topical Heading	Marine animals—Study and teaching.
690	Local Subject Heading	Octopus—Behavior.
710	Corporate Name added entry	North American National University Science Department, issuing body.
856	Electronic location and access	http://www.dailyoctopus.nanu.edu

Example 8
Electronic Item Practice Answers

MARC Tag	RDA Element	Field Entry
	Mode of issuance	i
	Local call number	597.92
245	Title Proper, Other Title Information, Statement of Responsibility	Turtle Watchers International
264	Place of Publication, Publisher's Name, Publication Date	Hampton Beach, New York : Turtle Watchers International, [2015]
264	Copyright Date	©2015.
300	Extent, Illustrations, Dimensions	1 online resource : digital, sound, color illustrations.
336	Content Type	text
336	Content Type	still image

(Continued)

Example 8 *(Continued)*

MARC Tag	RDA Element	Field Entry
336	Content Type	sounds
336	Content Type	two-dimensional moving image
337	Media Type	computer
338	Carrier Type	online resource
505	Formatted Contents Note	East—West—Weekly Watch—Write!—Donate!
520	Summary Note	Organizational website for Turtle Watchers International, a group monitoring turtle behavior and migration on the east and west coasts of the United States.
650	Sears Topical Heading	Turtles—Behavior.
710	Corporate Name Entry	Turtle Watchers International, issuing body.
856	Electronic location and access	http://www.turtlewatchers.org

Example 9
Electronic Item Practice Answers

MARC Tag	RDA Element	Field Entry
	Mode of issuance	I
	Local call number	641.5.
245	Title Proper, Other Title Information, Statement of Responsibility	Black Cat Recipe Barn / Black Cat Creations.
264	Place of Publication, Publisher's Name, Publication Date	Los Angeles : Black Cat Creations, [2014]
264	Copyright Date	©2014.
300	Extent, Illustrations, Dimensions	1 online resource : color illustrations.
336	Content Type	text
336	Content Type	still image
337	Media Type	computer
338	Carrier Type	online resource
505	Formatted contents note	Breakfast—Lunch—Dinner—Dessert.
520	Summary Note	Companion website to the famous Los Angeles restaurant, the Black Cat; it features recipes for favorite restaurant dishes.
650	Sears Topical Heading	Cooking. Restaurants—California.
710	Corporate Name added entry	Black Cat Creations, issuing body.

Example 10
Electronic Item Practice Answers

MARC Tag	RDA Element	Field Entry
	Mode of issuance	i
	Local call number	027.8
022	Identifying Number	0317–8471
245	Title Proper, Other Title Information, Statement of Responsibility	The Modern School Librarian / by the Modern Association of School Librarians (MASL)

MARC Tag	RDA Element	Field Entry
264	Place of Publication, Publisher's Name, Publication Date	Chicago, Illinois : Modern Association of School Librarians (MASL), [2014]
264	Copyright Date	©2014.
300	Extent, Illustrations, Dimensions	1 online resource (70 pages) : digital, sound, color illustrations.
336	Content Type	text
336	Content Type	still image
336	Content Type	two-dimensional moving image
337	Media Type	computer
338	Carrier Type	online resource
490	Series Statement	Mobile librarian issue ; volume 12, issue 7
520	Summary Note	MSL features innovative librarians and programming ideas throughout the United States.
650	Sears Topical Heading	School libraries—Associations.
710	Corporate Name Added Entry	Modern Association of School Librarians, publisher.
830	Series Added Entry Uniform Title	Mobile librarian issue ; volume 12, issue 7.
856	Electronic location and access	http://www.masl.org/msl

CHAPTER 10 ANSWERS

Example 6
Streaming Item Practice Answers

MARC Tag	RDA Element	Field Entry
	Mode of issuance	m
	Local call number	598
245	Title Proper, Other Title Information, Statement of Responsibility	The Wildlife Society Presents : Songbirds of the South Migration Update / produced by The Wildlife Society Songbird productions.
264	Place of Publication, Publisher's Name, Publication Date	Atlanta, Georgia : The Wildlife Society Songbird Productions, [2015]
264	Copyright Date	©2015.
300	Extent, Illustrations, Dimensions	1 online resource (30 min.) : digital, sound, color.
336	Content Type	two-dimensional moving image
336	Content Type	spoken word
336	Content Type	still image
337	Media Type	Computer
338	Carrier Type	online resource
520	Summary Note	Weekly migration update 21 covers the South's species of songbirds migration to Florida.
650	Sears Topical Heading	Birds—United States. Birds—Southern states. Birdsongs.
710	Corporate Name added entry	Wildlife Society Songbird Productions, production company.
856	Electronic location and access	http://www.wls.org/SOSreport

Example 7
Streaming Item Practice Answers

MARC Tag	RDA Element	Field Entry
	Mode of issuance	m
	Local call number	949.4
245	Title Proper, Other Title Information, Statement of Responsibility	Michelindamin's Motoring Tours the Alps with Franz and Fritz / Produced by Michelindamin Motoring.
250	Edition Statement	
264	Place of Publication, Publisher's Name, Publication Date	New York : Paris : Michelindamin Motoring, [2014]
264	Copyright Date	©2014.
300	Extent, Illustrations, Dimensions	1 online resource (1 video file (30 min.)) : digital, sound, color.
336	Content Type	two-dimensional moving image
336	Content Type	spoken word
337	Media Type	computer
338	Carrier Type	online resource
520	Summary Note	Michelindamin's Motoring tours the Swiss Alps with local tour guides Franz and Fritz Frankenthaler. The program highlights the sights and sounds of the region and reviews the best spots for motor camping.
651	Sears Geographic Heading	Switzerland—Description and Travel.
700	Name Added Entry	Frankenthaler, Franz, 1980-, actor.
700	Name Added Entry	Frankenthaler, Fritz, 1980-, actor.
710	Corporate Name Added Entry	Michelindamin Motoring, production company.
856	Electronic location and access	http://www.michelindamin.com/alps

Example 8
Streaming Item Practice Answers

MARC Tag	RDA Element	Field Entry
	Mode of issuance	m
	Local call number	B Landers 2015
245	Title Proper, Other Title Information, Statement of Responsibility	Turtle Watchers International Salute to George Landers / Turtle Watchers International Video Productions.
264	Place of Publication, Publisher's Name, Publication Date	Hampton Beach, New York : Turtle Watchers International, [2015]
264	Copyright Date	©2015.
300	Extent, Illustrations, Dimensions	1 online resource (1 video file (60 min.)) : digital, sound, color.
336	Content Type	two-dimensional moving image
336	Content Type	spoken word
336	Content Type	still image

MARC Tag	RDA Element	Field Entry
336	Content Type	performed music
337	Media Type	computer
338	Carrier Type	online resource
520	Summary Note	Video production features a biography of George Landers (1945–2014), famous turtle scientist and founding father of Turtle Watchers International. The program includes video clips, narration by scientist Leonard Nimrod, historical color photographs, and a musical performance by the Turtle Time band.
600	Personal Name Heading	Landers, George, 1945–2014.
650	Sears Topical Heading	Scientists—Biography.
700	Personal Name Added Entry	Nimrod, Leonard, narrator.
710	Corporate Name Added Entry	Turtle Watchers International, production company.
710	Corporate Name Added Entry	Turtle Time band, performer.
856	Electronic location and access	http://www.turtlewatchers.org/GeorgeLanders

Example 9
Streaming Item Practice Answers

MARC Tag	RDA Element	Field Entry
	Mode of issuance	m
	Local call number	597.8
245	Title Proper, Other Title Information, Statement of Responsibility	The Frog Chronicles Podcast 15 / produced by the Wildlife Society.
264	Place of Publication, Publisher's Name, Publication Date	[Washington, D.C.] : The Wildlife Society Audio Productions, [2015]
264	Copyright Date	©2015.
300	Extent, Illustrations, Dimensions	1 online resource (1 audio file (12 min.)) : digital, sound.
336	Content Type	spoken word
337	Media Type	computer
338	Carrier Type	online resource
490	Series Statement	The Frog Chronicles ; Podcast 15
520	Summary Note	The Wildlife Society weekly podcast for upper elementary students focusing specifically on frog habitats and behavior.
521	Target audience note	Elementary students.
650	Sears Topical Heading	Frogs—Behavior.
710	Corporate Name added entry	Wildlife Society Audio Productions, production company.
830	Series Added Entry Uniform Title	Frog Chronicles Podcast.
856	Electronic location and access	http://www.wls.org/frogchronicles/Pondpod15

Example 10
Streaming Item Practice Answers

MARC Tag	RDA Element	Field Entry
	Mode of issuance	m
	Local call number	794.2
245	Title Proper, Other Title Information, Statement of Responsibility	Bobbie Fish Says : OPEN LIKE A PRO! / Wildchess Productions, Inc.
264	Place of Publication, Publisher's Name, Publication Date	Norcross, Georgia : Wildchess Inc., [2013]
264	Copyright Date	©2013.
300	Extent, Illustrations, Dimensions	1 online resource (1 video file (20 min.)) : digital, sound, color.
336	Content Type	two-dimensional moving image
336	Content Type	spoken word
337	Media Type	computer
338	Carrier Type	online resource
520	Summary Note	Chess master Bobbie Fish narrates this program on winning with wild and aggressive opening moves.
650	Sears Topical Heading	Chess—Strategic aspects.
700	Name added entry	Fish, Robert, 1972-, narrator.
710	Corporate Name added entry	Wildchess Productions, Inc., production company.
856	Electronic location and access	http://www.wildchess.com/wildopeners

Glossary

AACR—the Anglo American Cataloging Rules were an outgrowth of the Paris Principles and became the set of rules used when creating catalog records for all types of items.

Acquisitions module—an ILS module used for ordering, receiving, and paying for library materials from library vendors.

ALA—the largest professional library organization in the world. The Library of Congress and the American Library Association serve as coordinators for establishing cataloging policies and procedures.

Alternative classification—classification systems that do not use either the DDC or LC systems in their library organization. Typically, libraries with alternative classification use a "bookstore" or "child-centered" model.

Authority files—a component of a library catalog listing the names and subject headings used for assigning subject headings to items in the catalog.

Authority module—this module uses the catalog database to maintain the consistency of headings used in describing bibliographic materials.

Baconian system—comprises the three human faculties of memory, imagination, and reason, which are identified with three main intellectual disciplines: historical sciences, the poetical sciences, and philosophy.

BIBFRAME standard—developed by the Library of Congress, BIBFRAME is a standard for bibliographic records, which is more compatible with relational databases now being used in automated catalog systems.

Bibliographic description—creating a descriptive record for an item in a library catalog based on professional standards.

Bibliographic universe—the term used to describe all the recorded knowledge in existence that can be included in a library catalog.

Bookstore model—classification system that uses genres and subject headings used by the Book Industry Study Group to organize items in the library.

Call number—the library notation system used to find an item's exact location on the shelf that combines the item's classification number, publication date, and occasionally a "Cutter number," which is a code created from the first letters of an author's surname.

Carrier Type—RDA core element describing the format in which information is delivered, including volume, audio disk, videodisk, online resource, and more.

Catalog—a list of items in a library.

Catalog in Publication (CIP)—catalog information listed on the verso or inside page of every printed item cataloged by the Library of Congress.

Catalog module—the module of an ILS used to create, store, retrieve, and manage bibliographic records.

Circulation module—module of an ILS used by library staff for managing the lending, return, renewal, holds of library materials, and user fines and fees for lost items.

Classification—a process of assigning a discipline or class to an item using a prescribed system of letters and numbers such as the Library of Congress or DDC systems.

Cloud-based ILS—ILS hosted on the Internet; the hardware is managed locally, while the software and information databases are managed through the ILS vendor as a subscription service.

Content type—RDA core element describing the form information takes on the item including text, still image, spoken word, performed music, two-dimensional moving image, three-dimensional image, and more.

Controlled vocabulary—a precise list of terms or subject headings applied to each information item when it is being cataloged.

Copy cataloging—cataloging procedure involving importing catalog records into the local system from a source provided by the library's book vendor or from another library, which are then matched with the information on the local item, edited, and added to the library's Online Public Access Catalog.

Core RDA elements—elements of a catalog required that RDA rules require; core elements include: title, statement of responsibility, edition statement, numbering of serials, publication/production/manufacture/copyright date statement, series statement, identifier for the manifestation, carrier type, and extent.

Cutter number—notation code comprising the letters in an author's name used in call numbers to assist with ordering items by author on the shelf.

Cutter's *Rules for a Dictionary Catalog*—rules itemizing the function of the library catalog to allow the user to find an item when the author, title, or subject is known; find what the library holdings are in relation to a given author, title, or subject; and assist with the choice of an item based on the edition, format, or character of an item.

Delimiters—subfield codes that are part of a machine-readable cataloging record (MARC) that identify different parts of the information being entered in the field. In most catalog programs, delimiters are preceded by a pipe mark | or a dollar sign $.

Dewey Decimal Classification (DDC)—a classification system based on the Baconian order of knowledge; uses numbers with three decimal places; the DDC has 10 main classes from 000 to 900, summary tables for the hundred division numbered from 000 to 990, and thousands section that are ordered from 000 to 999.

Dewey summaries—number tables that provide an overview of the classification system, listing the 10 main classes, the hundreds divisions, and the thousand sections.

Directory—term used in MARC21 to refer to information for the computer program on the length, starting points, and tags for catalog records.

Discovery interfaces/services—a discovery interface works with the ILS to bring together all the different databases students can use to search for information into one search box.

Federated searching—search technology that allows users to use one search box for searching multiple information databases, linking users to print and electronic resources with one query.

Fields—term used in MARC21 to refer to the place for entering catalog information.

Folksonomies—classification scheme resulting from tagging activities developed by a large population of users as opposed to a small group of people.

Functional Requirements for Bibliographic Records (FRBR)—published in 1998, FRBR reflects the ability of the 21st-century library catalogs to retrieve not only items related to a user's search, but also links to different editions, formats, adaptations, and other variations of the item the user might also be interested in.

Functions of a library catalog—the basic functions of the library catalog are to find an item by its known characteristics, assign a unique location for each item in the catalog, and group like items together.

Indicator—each MARC tag has a two digit indicator number that provides additional information about specific aspects of that particular field

Information discovery system—a system for managing the increasing amount of information added to the library's holdings so that they may be easily found by the user

Information silo—an information environment in which students access information in different areas of the library information portal; student research activities in an information silo would use more than one source to locate information in different formats

Integrated Library System (ILS)—an information system for libraries comprised of different features or "modules" that assist the school librarian with all of the collection management activities in the library.

International Federation of Library Associations (IFLA)—the governing body over the current international cataloging standards.

International Standard for Bibliographic Description (ISBD)—an outgrowth of the Paris Principles and specifies in detail how items are to be described in catalog records.

ISO 23950:*Information Retrieval (Z39.50): Application Service Definition and Protocol Specification*, ANSI/NISO Z39.50; this standard enables users to search and retrieve catalog records from multiple library databases from remote locations.

Learning commons model—school library model in which programs and services focus on information needs of users in all formats; library services include information enquiry instructions, collaborative learning, and technology leadership.

Legacy systems—term referring to automated catalogs that typically limit search options to specific fields such as subject, author, title, or keyword in title, and results are displayed in textual form.

Library automation system—also referred to as an integrated library system or automated library system, a library automation system is an information system that integrates different databases for managing the functions of the library.

Library of Congress (LOC)—much of the standards and practices for cataloging and classification originated in the Library of Congress (LOC), which, because it is the depository for copyrighted materials, is one of the world's largest libraries.

Library of Congress Card Catalog Service—a service provided by the Library of Congress that provides cataloging information on the verso or inside page of every printed item cataloged by the Library of Congress.

Library of Congress Classification System (LCC)—a classification system used in the Library of Congress, which comprises letters and numbers.

Library of Congress Subject Headings list (LCSH)—developed originally to manage the holdings of the U.S. Library of Congress, one of the world's largest libraries.

Library Services module—typically part of a next-generation catalog, the module ingrates different social networking applications such as blogs, RSS feeds, Pinterest, or Twitter feeds into the ILS in order to promote library services such as reference and readers' advisory.

MARBI—Machine-Readable Bibliographic Information Committee (MARBI) is responsible for the MARC standard, which specifies the structure of a catalog record and how the record is interpreted by a computer program for display; the current MARC standard is MARC21.

MARC (Machine-readable cataloging record)—computer records used in online catalogs that instruct the computer how to display the catalog record in the OPAC.

MARC Standard—the MARC format is the standard for computer library records across the globe. The different tags, fields, and indicators in a MARC record instruct the computer to display information in a particular way in the OPAC.

MARC view—catalog module utility that allows the cataloger to enter information by MARC tag, to make sure that they are including accurate information in the appropriate fields.

Media type—RDA element describing the means by which the item is made accessible for the user including unmediated, computer, audio, video, and more.

Mode of Issuance—RDA core element describing the manner in which the information is delivered including single unit, multipart monograph, serial, and integrating resource.

National Defense Education Act of 1958—a federal act that brought a trove of resources to schools in the math and science areas that required organization.

National Elementary and Secondary Education Act of 1965—the federal act that brought a trove of resources to schools related to promoting literacy.

Next-generation library catalogs—cutting-edge automated catalog systems that take advantage of the ability of the Internet to connect information portals, analyze and display information in different ways, and create collaborative participatory communities for sharing information.

OCLC—the Online Computer Library Center provides an organizing and coordinating function for creating and sharing catalog records that meet international and national standards.

OPAC (Online Public Access Catalog)—the feature of an automated catalog system that displays the catalog records associated with the library's holdings.

Open-Source ILS—software programs that use programming code freely available for programmers to create anything they want, including an ILS.

Original cataloging—cataloging procedure in which all of the information about an item is entered into the catalog module.

Paris Principles—international cataloging standards established in 1961 to standardize how items are described in a catalog record.

Preferred source of information—the location RDA requires for information that is used for identifying information for the catalog record, typically the title page for printed items, the cover or container for audiovisual items, or the website home page for Internet items.

Recording—cataloging procedure where information is entered into the catalog record using RDA prescribed terminology, notation, and formatting.

Record leader—term used in MARC21 to refer to computer code providing instructions for the computer program in how to display the catalog record.

Reporting module—an ILS module used to compile library statistics about circulation and use of collection, strategic analysis, review of library, and inventory activities.

Resource Description and Access (RDA)—the latest standard for cataloging library materials; its intent is to expand the range of materials that can be included in a library catalog to electronic and cloud-based items.

Sears List of Subject Headings (Sears)—developed by a single librarian, Minnie Earl Sears in 1923 to manage the smaller holdings of school and public libraries; the Sears list is based on LCSH headings but with fewer compound headings and less technical terminology.

Segmentation marks—either a prime ' or a forward slash / within a call number to show where the number can be shortened or lengthened.

Serials module—not commonly found in school library ILS, this module manages serials the library holds such as magazines and journals.

Shelf list—a feature of a library catalog that lists items as they are arranged on the shelf by classification.

Social tagging—activity in which users add their own descriptive terms to websites, pictures, catalog record, or other items found on the Internet Tag governance, the systematic use of tags for describing material primarily found online.

Software-as-a service or Saas Model—cloud-based subscription library automation services.

Subject analysis—the task of assigning subject terms that describe the most important facets of an item using a standard list of subject terms otherwise known as a "controlled vocabulary."

Tag—each MARC field is labeled with a three-digit number that denotes a different piece of bibliographic information such as the author's name, title, publication information, and description.

Tag cloud—Web 2.0 applications that allow tagging and compile the result of tagging activities in a visual display, with the popularity of words denoted by the size of the words.

Transcription—cataloging procedure where information is entered into the catalog record as it appears on the preferred source of information.

Uncontrolled vocabulary—a list of terms that groups add to without any overarching control or conscious decision making regarding what terms are added or deleted from the list.

Universal bibliographic control—the goal for published items to be cataloged promptly and made internationally accessible.

Universal Decimal Classification system (UDC)—a three-digit system using a similar set of main classes as the Dewey system designed for collections containing works in multiple languages.

Warehouse model—the school library model in which programs and services focus on the print collection and basic library organization.

Work mark—notation system using the first letter of the book's title that assists with ordering items by the same author then by title.

WorldCat—one of the world's largest online resource discovery systems maintained by the OCLC.

Z39.50 protocol—maintained by the Library of Congress. Z39.50 refers to the International Standard Metis—Child-centered classification system using user-generated whole-word categories for fiction and nonfiction.

References

"About OCLC." (2015). Retrieved from https://www.oclc.org/about.en.html

Adamich, T. (July/August 2013). Making and managing metadata: Sears Subject Heading List: A tool ahead of its time. *Technicalities*, 33(4): 8–11.

American Library Association. Association for Library Collections and Technical Services. Committee on Cataloging: Description and Access. http://www.ala.org/alcts/mgrps/camms/cmtes/ats-ccscat

Baker, K. (November 13, 2012). Folksonomies and social tagging. *The Idaho librarian.* https://theidaholibrarian.wordpress.com/2012/11/13/social-tagging-2012/

Barton, J. & Mak, L. (2012). Old hopes, new possibilities: next-generation catalogues and the centralization of access. *Library Trends*, 61(1): 83–106.

Bibliographic Framework Initiative. (2015). http://www.loc.gov/bibframe/faqs/

Bilal, D. (2014). *Library automation: Core concepts and practical systems analysis*, 3rd ed. Santa Barbara, CA: ABC-CLIO.

Bowman, J. (2005). *Essential Dewey*. New York: Neal Schuman.

Breeding, M. (2007). WorldCat local. *Library Technology Reports*, 43(4): 33–37. Retrieved from Academic Search Premier.

Breeding, M. (2010). *Next-Gen Library Catalogs (THE TECH SET® #1)*. New York: Neal-Schuman Publishers (in cooperation with the Library Information and Technology Association, a division of the American Library Association).

Breeding, Marshall. (2014). Library Systems Report 2014: Competition and strategic cooperation. *American Libraries*, 45(5): 21–33. http://www.americanlibrariesmagazine.org/article/library-systems-report-2014

Bristow, B. & Farrar, C. (Eds.) (2014). *Sears List of subject headings*, 21st ed. New York: H.W. Wilson.

Broughton, V. (2004). *Essential classification*. New York: Neal-Schuman Publishers.

Buchter, H. (2013). Dewey vs. genre throwdown. *Knowledge Quest*, 42(2): 48–55.

Casey, M. (2007). Looking toward catalog 2. In Nancy Courtney (ed.) *Library 2.0 and beyond*, Westport, CT: Libraries Unlimited.

Chan, L. (2007). *Cataloging and classification: An introduction*, 3rd ed. Lanham, MD: Scarecrow Press.

"Creates Standards That Matter," American Library Association, March 9, 2010. Retrieved September 3, 2015, from http://www.ala.org/membership/whataladoes/createstandards

Current IFLA Standards. (2014). Retrieved from http://www.ifla.org/node/8750

Cutter, C. (1876). *Rules for a dictionary catalog*. Washington, DC: Government Printing Office.

Dewey, M. (2012). *Abridged Dewey Decimal Classification and relative index*, 15th ed. Dublin, OH: OCLC.

Druin, A. (2005). What children can teach us: Developing digital libraries for children with children. *Library Quarterly*, 75: 20–41.

"Fascinating Facts," n.d. Retrieved from https://www.loc.gov/about/fascinating-facts/

Fiehn, B. (2007). Social networking through your library automation system: What librarians and vendors have to say. *Multimedia & Internet Schools*, 16(5): 28–31.

Fiehn, B. (2008). Social networking and your library OPAC! *Multimedia & Internet Schools*, 15(4): 27–29.

Fountain, J. (2011). Guidelines for standardized cataloging for children. In Intner, S., Fountain, J., & Weihs, J. *Cataloging correctly for kids: An introduction to the tools*. Chicago, IL: American Library Association.

Fountain, J. (2012). *Subject headings for school and public libraries: Bilingual fourth edition*. Santa Barbara, CA: Libraries Unlimited.

Fritz, D. (2011). Copy cataloging correctly. In Intner, S., Fountain, J., & Weihs, J. *Cataloging correctly for kids: An introduction to the tools*. Chicago, IL: American Library Association.

Front matter. (2007). In *Sears List of Subject Headings*, 19th ed. New York: H. W. Wilson. Retrieved from http://support.ebsco.com/help/index.php?help_id=DB:904

Functional Requirements for Bibliographic Records. (2009). Retrieved from http://www.ifla.org/publications/functional-requirements-for-bibliographic-records

Furrie, B. (2009). Understanding MARC bibliographic Machine Readable Cataloging. Washington, DC: Library of Congress. Retrieved from http://www.loc.gov/marc/umb/

Haynes, E., Fountain, J., & Zwierski, M. (2015). *Unlocking the mysteries of cataloging: A workbook of examples*. Santa Barbara, CA: Libraries Unlimited.

Hutchinson, H., Rose, A., Bederson, B., Weeks, A., & Druin, A. (2005). The International Children's Digital Library: A case study in designing for a multilingual, multicultural, multi-generational audience. *Information Technology and Libraries*, 24(1): 4–12.

Intner, S. & Weihs, J. (2015). *Standard cataloging for school and public libraries*, 5th ed. Santa Barbara, CA: Libraries Unlimited.

Introduction. (2014). *Library of Congress List of Subject Headings*, 36th edition. Retrieved from http://www.loc.gov/aba/publications/FreeLCSH/lcshintro.pdf

Jacox, C., Margaret, M., Moll, M., Nimsakont, E., & Routt, D. (2014). *The RDA workbook: Learning the basics of Resource Description and Access*. Santa Barbara, CA: Libraries Unlimited.

Jameson, J. (2013). Dewey or don't we: A genre conversation begins. *Knowledge Quest*, 42(2): 10.

Joint Steering Committee (JSC), American Library Association (ALA), Canadian Library Association (CLA), Chartered Institute for Library and Information Professionals (CLIP, UK), Deutsch Nationalbibliotek, Library of Congress (LC). (2013). *RDA : Resource Description and Access : 2013 Revision*. Chicago, IL: American Library Association.

Kaplan, T., Giffard, S., Still-Schiff, J., & Dolloff, A. (2013). One size does not fit all: Creating a developmentally appropriate classification for your children's collection. *Knowledge Quest*, 42(2): 31–37.

Karpuk, D. (2008). *Kidzcat: A how to manual for cataloging children's materials and instructional resources*. Chicago, IL: Neal-Schuman.

Kelsey, M. (2014). *Cataloging for school libraries*. New York: Rowman & Littlefield.

Library of Congress Classification Outline. Retrieved from http://www.loc.gov/catdir/cpso/lcco/

Loertscher, D., Koechlin, C., & Zwaan, S. (2011). *The new learning commons where learners win! Reinventing school libraries and computer labs*. Salt Lake City, UT: Hi Willow Research.

Michie, J. & Holton, B. (2005). Fifty years of supporting children's learning: A history of public school libraries and Federal legislation from 1953 to 2000. Washington, DC: National Center for Education Statistics. Retrieved from http://nces.ed.gov/pubs2005/2005311.pdf

National Center for Educational Statistics. (2013). *Characteristics of public elementary and secondary school library media centers in the United States: Results from the 2011–12 Schools and Staffing Survey.* Retrieved from http://nces.ed.gov/pubs2013/2013315.pdf

OCLC. (2003). Dewey summaries. Dublin, OH, OCLC. Retrieved from http://www.oclc.org/DEWEY/resources/summaries/deweysummaries.pdf

Statement of International Cataloging Principles. (2012). Retrieved from http://www.ifla.org/publications/statement-of-international-cataloguing-principles

Sullivan, M. (2013). *Fundamentals of children's services.* Chicago, IL: American Library Association.

Tarulli, L. & Spiteri, L. (2012). Library catalogues of the future: A social space and collaborative tool? *Library Trends,* 61(1): 107–131.

Taylor, A. (2000). *Wynar's introduction to cataloging and classification,* 9th ed. Englewood, CO: Libraries Unlimited.

Taylor, A. (2004). *The organization of information,* 2nd ed. Westport, CT: Libraries Unlimited, Inc..

Wagner, A. (August 12, 2012). Dewey Decimal System gets check. *TribLive.* [Blog] http://trib.me/N1lmKn

Weihs, J. & Intner, S. (2009). *Beginning cataloging.* Santa Barbara, CA: Libraries Unlimited.

Welsh, A. & Bately, S. (2012). *Practical cataloguing: AACR, RDA and MARC 21.* London: Facet.

Index

Note: Page numbers in *italics* followed by *f* indicate figures and by *t* indicate tables

186   Index

About the Author

CYNTHIA HOUSTON is a professor in the Master of Science program in library media education at Western Kentucky University, Bowling Green, Kentucky. She has worked in library special collections and as a media specialist in Kentucky, Tennessee, and Illinois. Houston has written widely in professional journals and presented at state and national conferences.

Made in the USA
Middletown, DE
04 September 2020